Not Those People

Zak Maiden   LC Mickler

Not Those People

Finding
Recovery
Through
Redemption

gatekeeper press™

Columbus, Ohio

Not Those People: Finding Recovery Through Redemption

Published by Gatekeeper Press
2167 Stringtown Rd, Suite 109
Columbus, OH 43123-2989
www.GatekeeperPress.com

The cover design, interior formatting, typesetting, and editorial work for this book are entirely the product of the author. Gatekeeper Press did not participate in and is not responsible for any aspect of these elements.

Library of Congress Control Number: 2021943464

ISBN (hardcover): 9781662917592
ISBN (paperback): 9781662917608
eISBN: 9781662917615

Table of Contents

Introduction

Maybe you don't think that you would ever bend over a pool table in a basement and snort cocaine.

Maybe you don't think you would ever pick up a gun, point it at your skull, and pull the trigger.

Maybe you don't think you'd ever slash the tender flesh of your own arms.

Maybe you don't think you'd allow your molars to rot and your nasal passages to fold from substance abuse.

Maybe you've never been named an addict or had a label assigned to the depths of your hopelessness or the swinging of your moods from low to high.

Or maybe you have.

Maybe you've been the one with nostrils over a pool table or needles in your hand. Maybe you've touched the smooth inside of a trigger or fought to keep your wrists from flicking your steering wheel into the direction of oncoming traffic and the blackout that would follow.

Maybe you have been labeled or diagnosed with depression, anxiety, bipolar disorder, or drug addiction.

Maybe you've felt those labels sear into your being like a branding iron.

Those who know, know. Those who don't, can't seem to imagine.

Subjects on addiction and mental health are discussed by politicians, law enforcement, celebrities, doctors, and experts. The majority of people would like to think of someone like me as *the other people* - the ones who serve as the automatic lower rung of society, here to give everyone else the satisfaction of saying *at least I'm not like **those people***.

All the while, average teenagers from blue-collar families are snorting drugs in parking lots after school. Stay-at-home moms pour a fourth glass of wine in front of the television after tucking the children in bed. Pills are popped for injuries that were gone long ago. The college student battles debilitating anxiety. The coffee barista doesn't know why she feels like she can conquer the world one day and can't get out of bed the next. And the high school student isn't telling anyone how the edge of the rooftop and the oblivion below pulls at her like a magnet. I am among these.

We are not *those people.*

We are not violent criminals or shiny celebrities.

We are not on street corners or in trap houses.

We are every day, hardworking, average people who are fighting battles in the dark. And that's why I want to tell my story. Because it's time to stop being afraid of being ***those people.***

So, hi. I'm Zak Maiden.

Your son,

Your boyfriend,

Your brother,

Your friend,

You,

The Recovering Addict

Chapter 1: The Water That Tasted Funny

Has anyone ever asked you what your earliest memory is? Your mind digs and searches, trying to find your first preserved moment of consciousness.

You probe until you feel vague impressions swirling in the mind, like the remnants of a dream that lingers for the first few moments after sleep. There, a memory. You reach for it, hold onto it, examine it. But then you begin to wonder if you are actually holding onto a recollection or simply imagining a story you've been told a hundred times.

And so, you keep searching until you find a memory with substance, color, and sight. A memory that you can grab and hold on to. The first one that you know without a doubt is yours and yours alone. This is the marker that begins the recording of your awareness.

For me, this marker took place in the upstairs bedroom of my parents' home in Millersburg, Pennsylvania, when I was in second grade.

That night, I couldn't sleep. I tried to shut my eyes, thinking that if I kept them closed for long enough, I'd finally drift off. But then all I could think about was how much I wanted to open them. So, I did, after what felt like an eternity, but was probably only a matter of seconds.

I felt hot and kicked off my blanket. And then I felt cold and covered myself back up again. I laid on my belly and then on my back. Neither one made me feel like sleeping. I opened my eyes, thinking that the shadows looked weird on the wall. Why are there a hundred spots for something to hide when it's dark?

My room was in an attic. I remember hearing my mom describe our house as "Victorian" while talking to one of her friends, and I wasn't sure what that meant. All I knew was that my room was at the top of the staircase - smashed right up against my brother's. He is seven years older than I am, which made him fourteen on that night. I thought he was cool and tough. Everything I wanted to be.

I looked around my room while I waited for sleep to come. I looked at the big bookshelf on one of my walls. I looked at my window and considered getting up and looking outside to see if anyone was on the street. I liked throwing things out of my window to see if I could hit a car without anyone realizing it was me. I told myself that it was probably too late for people to be walking or driving around and stayed in bed.

I really did try to stay in bed and fall asleep that night. But, when you are young and sleep refuses to pick you up and speedily transport you through the long hours of the night, it feels like staring down a black eternity. That night I just couldn't stand it any longer.

So, I sat up, and I wondered if my brother was awake, too. I had to tell someone that I couldn't sleep. I knew he might get annoyed or angry with me for bothering him, but it seemed like a better alternative than laying in my hot-cold bed forever. I tiptoed across the floor and to the door of his room, which didn't take long. I tried to open the door quietly, but every sound rang out like a megaphone through the quietness. Why does everything sound louder when it's dark?

The door made a thudding noise when I shut it behind me, but my brother didn't move from his bed. His wall was covered in artwork of all of his favorite singers and bands, but it was too dark to see anything. In just a few short years, I would sneak into his room when he wasn't around to look at the CD covers and my favorite would be Foxy Brown. I would think she was pretty and stare at her provocative clothes until I could imagine her without any clothes on at all. But that night my young mind was only filled with thoughts of wanting to sleep.

I walked past my brother's shelf of baseball cards, trophies, and shot glasses that looked like tiny cups, all the way to his bed.

"Pssst. Are you awake?" I whispered.

He made a groaning sound and rolled over but didn't answer me. So, I tapped on his leg and tried to make my voice a little stronger.

"I can't sleep," I said again, louder this time.

"Go away, Zak," he said.

"I'm trying to sleep. I promise. But I CAN'T," I said.

Finally, he sat up. He rubbed his eyes, flipped on his lamp, and looked at me standing at the foot of his bed. He paused for a few moments without saying anything and then grabbed a clear jar off of his nightstand, leaned forward, and handed it to me.

"Here, take a drink of this, Zak," he said. "This is special, flavored water. It will help you fall asleep."

I took the jar from him and gulped down the clear liquid. It didn't taste like water at all. It was sour and burned when I swallowed. I coughed a little bit but held onto the jar for several minutes. And then I took another sip. And another.

A strange feeling went through my body. That burning sensation tingled the back of my throat even after the liquid had finished sliding down. My arms and legs felt like noodles and my mind felt just as mushy. I don't remember how long I sat there or how many drinks of special water I took. But I remember that when I tried to walk, I felt wobbly and imbalanced.

"I think I need to get mom," I said. "I don't feel so good."

My brother shook his head vigorously.

"Don't get mom. Just come lay down right here," he said.

I crawled into his bed and pulled a blanket over my body. Suddenly, I just wanted to lay very, very still. I told myself that if I closed my eyes the strange feelings would pass.

I thought about the flavored water in the jar.

I thought about wanting my mom.

Just imagine you're floating, I said to myself.

And then I went to sleep.

Chapter 2: Impersonating Myself

After my recollection of that night, the night I had alcohol for the first time, memories of my childhood come in spurts. They aren't extraordinary or even linear, but I want to share them with you, because more than likely, they will remind you of your own childhood. People rarely think about what an addict was like as a child. People don't realize that we were once the kid on the bus, the child at the dinner table, and the teammate on the basketball court. I will show you my evil, my ugly, in the pages to come. But I will also show you my innocent and my pure. I want you to see me in my entirety. Because that's the only way to tell you the whole truth. Because I was the child who brushed ice cream off his nose before cocaine.

And in many ways, this story is more about that child, The Real Zak, than it ever was about the addict.

I was shy as a kid. Painfully shy. I wanted to be liked, as everyone does, but I found it hard to feel included. It seemed that other kids knew some secret key to making friends. Like they had a special superpower that made everyone like them and want to be around them. I wanted to be like that - to fit in, to play well with the others. But no matter how hard I tried, I felt like a puzzle piece that didn't fit. The other kids would say something hilarious and everyone would laugh. I wanted to make them laugh too, but I felt nervous at the mere thought of all those eyes on me.

In second grade, I saw the other children gather on the basketball court to play a game during recess. I ran over as fast as I could and squeezed into the huddle. The hot sun shone down on us and I watched two drops of sweat slide down one of the other boy's cheeks, as if in a race to see who could get down the slope first.

Two of the popular boys stood in front of our group and started taking turns picking people to be on their team. I stood tall, waiting to hear my name. Suddenly, one of them pointed straight at me. My heart leapt and I took a step forward to run to his side until someone behind me caught my shoulder.

"Not you, dummy. He meant me," he said. And then he laughed at my eagerness.

I felt humiliated and embarrassed. I stood still and waited for my turn to be chosen. I was the last one. I tried to act like it didn't bother me, but it did. It bothered me a lot.

It took a long time for my turn to play to come around. When it finally came, I felt nervous and shy. My heart pounded as I stood up and everything around me seemed to swirl. My pulse throbbed as if it was beating right in my eardrum and the sound of my playmates seemed far away. My jaw tightened and locked into place. The kids looked at me and I looked back, suddenly realizing that I wasn't really sure how to play. I tried to do the things that I saw everyone else doing, but I felt awkward and I didn't do anything right. I bumped into my own teammates and stepped on people's feet. I could see the looks on their faces. I could see the eyes rolling. I knew they were annoyed. It wasn't long before someone else took the ball and I never got another turn to play.

Another snapshot transports me to nights spent in the upstairs area that overlooked the bar my parents partially owned and managed. I grew up in a rural area of Pennsylvania, barely an hour away from the famous Lancaster county, home of the Amish. The rich landscape of mountains, valleys, and rolling fields is broken only by small towns sprinkled throughout. These small towns are filled with quaint streets and shops - reminiscent of happier, simple times, like Mayberry in *The Andy Griffith Show*. The outlying farmland is nothing short of picturesque. Rolling green hills, orchards, and pristine Amish farms with clothes flapping on clotheslines in the wind and fields golden and glowing in the sunlight.

The town of Millersburg is where I spent the majority of my childhood. It is filled with good-hearted, hardworking men and women, the kind of people on whose back America was built. People who work with pride and don't shy away from a little sweat and elbow grease. And with a population of about 3,000, everyone seems to know each other. But what our little town has in natural beauty and antique charm, it lacks in the way of entertainment or activities. People there work hard by day and drink hard by night. Bars, drinking, and a little gambling are among the few activities offered in Millersburg, except for maybe a church service. And so the six bars that line the small main street are the gathering places, the social hub of the town.

I remember riding with my dad to his bar in the valley on nights that he had to work late. Oftentimes, I would get bored and wish that I could go back home to my own bed. Other times, I didn't mind it so much. There was an RC Cola cooler right when you walked through the door. This wasn't the drink of choice for most people who came into the bar, which meant that it was always stocked with cold soda for me. There was a dart board on the wall, which might have been fun if I was any good at the game. I was terrible at it, no matter how hard I tried.

But to me, even better than the RC Cola cooler or the dart board was getting to play with the Megatouch machine. When it was still early in the evening, before the bar was filled with people ready to drink, I was allowed to play on the machine. I'd spend every minute I could before my dad would send me to the little back room where I would be expected to stay until he was ready to head home. I knew the words to all of my favorite songs and I would play them as loud as I could. They made me feel happy. Sometimes, when Mom wasn't there, I would play the X-rated, photo finder game so that I could see the naked ladies. In that dark and smoky room, the sound of music was a bright spot for me, almost as if the songs were shining sunlight into the room.

In the darkness of the main room stood a curved bar and I would watch people gather around it from the top of the stairs where I spent most of time on nights my parents worked late. Sometimes, I would watch and wonder how all those people could sit there for so long. I didn't understand why they just sat there, sipping drinks, not ordering

anything to eat for hours. I thought of how much I hated waiting for
the waitress to bring out the food when my parents took me out to
eat. That's why I loved going to The Nickel or Wayne's, two of the
local restaurants that always brought free bread to snack on while you
waited for food to come. I couldn't imagine sitting for hours, drinking
and not eating, with no free bread in sight. The whole thing sounded
miserable and looked miserable through the lens of my young eyes.
Sometimes, the people would talk around the bar. Sometimes they
wouldn't. But they would always stay there for hours. Where else was
there to go?

I remember listening to the sound of people laughing loudly
downstairs and I'd wish that I knew what was so funny so I could
laugh too. Everyone seemed to laugh more the later it got. But I wasn't
allowed to go past the bottom of the stairs when it was that late. Some
nights, I would sneak into the main room and watch people. If my dad
saw me he would send me straight back upstairs or into the back room
near the kitchen.

"Z-man!" he'd yell. "You know you're not supposed to be down
here."

I knew better than to disobey.

So, I'd return to the top of the stairs and wait for the long night to
end so I could return to my own bed at home, coloring in my coloring
books or playing with my collection of hunter green Army men.

From my earliest years, all the way up until fifth grade, I had a
mullet. Not a little, ratty excuse for one, but a thick, respectable one.
I was proud of it. That is until the other kids teased and called me a
girl. Then I felt self-conscious and shy, and I wondered if they would
like me more if I cut it. I wanted to belong, to be accepted into a tight-
knit friend group. But I couldn't seem to find an entry point. I had
two friends who liked to play games like Age of Empires and Warcraft
like I did, but everyone said we were nerdy and lame. Making friends
was not an easy thing for me and I envied other children who seemed
to do it effortlessly. I often felt shy and anxious, uncomfortable in

my own skin. So I tried hard to morph myself into something more acceptable. I tried changing the way I dressed or talked, hoping that this new version of myself would be someone who people would like, someone whose heart didn't pound and hands didn't get sweaty when people looked at him.

In sixth grade, I cut my hair. I was eager to get to school the next day, wondering what the kids would say when I walked in without my mullet. A couple of kids said, *"You look different,"* and I wasn't sure if that was good or bad. So I found some hair gel at the little department store in town, gel that turned your hair different colors. I showed up to school every day that year with a new hair color, hoping. I'm not even sure what I was hoping for. I was looking for an entrance into the world of people and friendships that everyone else seemed to automatically step into. I could never seem to find the door.

I often wondered what the other kids did after school. Every once in a while, one of my classmates invited me to play with them, but not often. Most afternoons, I played video games with my brother. We had one large Zenith TV and another tiny one. My brother's girlfriend gave him a PlayStation for Christmas and we played on it almost every day. I'd fix us both big cups of cold Pepsi to drink while we played. We had a *"secret recipe"* for what we believed to be the best cup of soda you've ever had. We'd pour maraschino cherry juice into the Pepsi and then put a cherry on top. We thought it was amazing and guzzled it by the gallons.

Sometimes, we would stop at the gas station and get candy. I liked the candy there, but not as much as the candy selection at the weekly auction a few miles from our house. The auction had everything. It was the place the farmers, butchers, and artisans would sell their goods. There were homemade crafts, butcher stands with fresh meat and poultry, eggs, fresh fruit and vegetables. And there was a whole booth with nothing but candy. It was amazing. When I was very small, my mom pushed me inside the store in a stroller and I stole a package of mini gumballs and started eating them. When she saw me, she was upset and marched back to the booth and returned it to the owner. I hadn't meant to do anything wrong; I just didn't understand. Isn't that how it usually goes? Isn't it often innocence that leads us down the first step of a destructive path?

Even though the gas station candy was not nearly as good as the candy from the auction, it was my constant companion through those afternoons of playing video games at home. I remember looking for a snack one day, opening up all the cabinets around the kitchen as if new snacks might have appeared since the last time I looked. Most of the cabinets were stuffed with household items we didn't use, but one was filled with bottles of all shapes and sizes. They were the same kind of bottles that lined the wall of the bar. I had never noticed them in the house before. I didn't realize we had our own collection.

Another day in sixth grade, I discovered a pack of cigarettes on my mom's dresser. No one was home, so I grabbed one. I knew where the lighter was in the top drawer in the kitchen and wasted no time in lighting up the cigarette. I put it between my fingers, lifted it to my mouth and pressed it between my lips. I thought of my brother's friends, trying to remember exactly how they looked when they smoked. I had seen them do it before, when my brother and a group of his friends picked me up from school. I would sit in the backseat and they would drive into a parking lot and then light up. The smell that filled the car was thick but they looked happy and cool with puffs of gray swirling out of their mouths.

I lit the cigarette. I didn't breathe in and smoke didn't fill up my mouth like when my brother's friends did it. But, for just a moment, I felt like maybe I could be them. Like someday, I would grow up to be cool, confident, and happy like they seemed to be.

When I was alone, I would often pretend or make believe in my mind. And then when I was around people again, I'd feel awkward and change my voice or act differently. I tried out a variety of voices and mannerisms as if I were in a dressing room, trying on clothing to wear. Some years I dressed preppy and impeccable, with all the best clothes from American Eagle, and grew my hair out. But then the kids called me gay. I wasn't gay, but I quickly realized that people made assumptions based on looks. Another time, I spoke like a country hick for a while. But it didn't stick and no one seemed to like me any better for all the effort.

When no one was around, I would continue to pretend. I would pretend to be a superhero, a villain, or a strong character from a movie. But the pretending I did alone felt different from the act I did in front of people. Alone, I felt invincible. Like I could do anything. Like I could be the hero or the life of the party. And for those few minutes, I didn't feel self-conscious. Or anxious. I felt free. Just like the day I grabbed a cigarette and pretended to be like my brother's friends.

I remember going to my Gram's house for Wednesday family dinner for most of my childhood. She would cook mashed potatoes, corn on the cob, duck, and hot bread rolls. That smell would envelop me when I walked into the room and it was so good that sometimes I thought I would burst.

One night everyone sat down, ready to eat, but my dad wasn't there. He had gone out on the front porch to take a phone call on his new cell phone. He took it everywhere with him and in those days we were all enamored with the novelty of that shiny device. But my grandmother wasn't going to have it. She marched her tiny frame outside and yelled at him to get off his phone and come and sit down to eat. I expected him to yell back at her, because *nobody* ordered my dad around. But he clicked off his phone immediately and came and sat down at the table like an obedient kid. I almost smiled watching someone put him in his place like that. I almost smiled, but I didn't.

From sixth through ninth grade, most of my memories revolved around the local swimming pool where I spent the majority of my free time after school and during the summer. My mom would often drop me off for the afternoon and give me $20 for food at the concession stand. At first, I jumped in the pool, harassed the lifeguard, and stared at the girls in bikinis like all the other boys.

But then a group of eighth graders, who also went to my school, approached me and started talking to me. I felt nervous at first, but they were friendly, disarming, and full of smiles. I couldn't believe that they actually liked me enough to come over and talk with me. I found myself laughing and having a good time. My own classmates called to me, begging me to come and play with them. But it wasn't often a sixth grader gets the attention of the older kids. I waved away my friends and stood tall in the midst of the cool kids.

And then one of them told me that he had forgotten his wallet. He was bummed that he didn't have any money to buy food. Eager to please my new friends, I offered him the $20 my mom gave me so that he could buy himself something. I had my eye on a plate of nachos and an ice cream bar, the look of happiness on his face when I gave him the money was worth going hungry. The whole group high-fived me. I felt happy and accepted, something I had craved for a long time.

A few days later, I went to the pool again. The same group of eighth graders came walking by. I smiled and approached eagerly but no one smiled back. They laughed at me and teased me instead, reducing me to the fool, a spectacle in front of everyone. I felt stupid for thinking that we were actually friends, for trusting them. I vowed that I would never do it again.

But then a few days later the group approached me, all smiles. They patted me on the back and we chatted. Maybe I had it all wrong. Maybe they were my friends after all. After a few minutes, they told me of another series of unfortunate events that had left them without any cash to buy food. Once again, I gave them the cash my mom had given me. And, once again, they smiled and pounded my back and let me hang out with them for the rest of the afternoon.

"You're the best Z-Man," they said.

And that made me feel good.

But a few days later they were back to teasing and bullying me as if we had never been friends. That is, until they needed money. And then they would pretend we were best friends again. This same cycle continued day after day, week after week, summer after summer.

Every year, I would promise myself that I wouldn't spend the whole summer giving them money like I had done the summer before. But the thought of acceptance, even for just a few moments was too enticing to turn them away. At times I actually thought that they were starting to like me. I would tell myself that it was because I was way cooler than I had been the year before. Better hair, better clothes. I'd give them my money and they would grin and high-five me like I was one of the gang. I'd tell myself that things were different this time, that it was me, not my money that they were after. But deep down, I knew the truth.

And I felt cheap, reduced to buying my entry into the world of friendship. But I didn't see any other way. The door didn't seem to open up for me like it did for everyone else and I was tired of peering through the window and watching the others, too tired of changing my persona and knocking at the door, hoping that somehow the newest version of myself would be welcomed inside.

I would watch my cousin at the pool and wish that I could be more like him. He looked happy and sure of himself, like he already knew exactly who he was and was comfortable with it. He would hang out with the people he liked and avoid the ones he didn't. He didn't seem to care what people thought. He was always laughing with the kids his own age while I found myself drawn back to the group of now ninth graders like a magnet. Sometimes I thought I was happy as I laughed and joked with them. But inevitably, they would tease me the following day until I felt embarrassed to even stand in front of them. Every time I showed up to the pool, I didn't know if I would find friends or a circle of bullies. This only compounded my social anxieties. I wished that I didn't care about them liking me. I wished I knew how to say no.

I wanted to be happy and friendly. Most of all, I wanted to stop feeling like I was impersonating myself. I wanted someone to tell me the right way to talk, joke, dress, and do my hair so that I would be accepted.

But try as I might, I never seemed to hit the mark. I couldn't seem to shake the feeling of discomfort in my own skin, the feeling that I didn't fit the mold, that I was somehow different.

And then one day, I had my first beer. A few of my friends from school came over to my house and we stumbled upon a cooler from a party that my parents had thrown several days before. We opened it up and found a pile of Budweisers inside. The ice had long melted and the beer was lukewarm, but we cracked them open and each took a can. We dared each other to drink it. The first sip on my tongue was a shock. It was horrible, bitter, and burned going down. I didn't let my disgust show. The boys looked on with respect as I took another generous gulp. "*Nobody likes a wimp,*" I told myself.

So I downed my can just like the others. We felt like real men that day, drinking beer from a cooler just like our fathers and older brothers did. Someday, we'd be the men at the local bars. Someday, we'd work hard to earn our nightly drinks. I only hoped by that time, I would actually like the taste.

After the last sip of beer was gone, I felt relaxed. We all laughed a little more than usual and I thought of the laughs that used to float up the stairs during those long nights I spent overlooking my dad's bar.

Suddenly, I didn't feel shy and I didn't feel anxious.

And for the first time, I understood why all those people came to sit at my dad's bar night after night.

Chapter 3: Meeting Z-Man

The first time I saw the glossy screen of my dad's trio palm pilot, I knew I had to have one. No one had phones with touchscreens like that in those days and I knew I'd be the talk of the school. I begged my parents to get me one and they finally did. I felt so cool and powerful as I punched away at the screen and showed my friends who stroked it with awe.

My friends weren't the only ones who noticed.

In my freshman year of high school, I leaned up against the bottom of the bleachers of our small local soccer field half watching the game, half poking around on my phone.

"Hey, Zak!"

I looked a few rows up to see a group of girls staring down at me. They were seniors and they were beautiful. Of course, all girls are beautiful when you're fifteen, but these girls seemed especially attractive. The faces looked familiar but I didn't know any of them well. The only girl I recognized was the one shouting my name. She was one of my brother's friends.

"Hey!" I said, unoriginally, and waved back, too stupid to figure out a way to keep the conversation going. I kept leaning on the bleachers, hoping my silence would scream a Fonzie-like coolness instead of the awkward paralysis I felt.

"We hear you got a new phone and we want to see it. Toss it over here!" she smirked.

I didn't normally hand out my phone, but in the mind of a high school boy, having pretty, older girls touch your phone is the next best thing to them touching you, so I tossed it their way without a second thought.

A large man above me in the stands blocked my view and I couldn't see what they did with it. I heard a few giggles and I took a sudden interested in the soccer game, trying to appear casual and unconcerned. Nobody likes the overly-eager guy craning his neck.

"Cool phone. Thanks for letting us take a look," said the girl who was my brother's friend as she handed it back.

"Sure, no problem," I said, trying to act natural.

I sat in silence for a bit and tried to focus on the game but my mind wandered toward the concession stand.

"You know what would make this game so much more interesting?"

"Talking to those girls."

"Well, are you gonna talk to them?"

"Hell no. I don't know what to say."

"Then how about a plate of salty chips with hot, creamy nacho cheese?"

"Yeah, that I can do."

These are the deep thoughts that probe the teenage male mind. I stood up and walked to the concession stand. As I stood in line, I heard a ding on my phone and looked down to see a text message flash onto the screen from an unknown number.

"Nice phone," it read.

I whipped my head around as if I was going to find some Russian spy in a dark hat lurking in some corner watching me. But no one was around except for the guy glopping processed cheese on chips and squirting mustard on hot dogs and a few hungry bystanders.

"*Who is this?*" I typed back.

"*This is Abbey. We just met on the stands. Just thought I'd text and say hi.*"

I re-read the message four times. My Russian spy hypothesis seemed more plausible than the idea that a pretty senior actually wanted my number.

"*No way. Who the fuck is this really?*"

So much for playing it cool. I waited for a text to come back with an admission to a prank from one of my buddies.

"*My name is Abbey and we literally just met on the stands. There were three of us sitting together, I was in the middle.*"

My mind flashed back to the group of girls smiling as they asked for my phone. The girl in the middle was sitting beside the friend of my brother, and she was beautiful.

I texted back with a lame stab at a joke and she responded with something cute and the texts flew back and forth. For the rest of the day. And the next. And the next.

"*Do you have Verizon?*" she messaged on day three.

"*No, I'm with Cingular.*"

"*Shit, I'm going to go over my text message limit. It's too bad you're not on Verizon so we could have unlimited messages.*"

Guess who became a faithful Verizon customer that week? That's right.

We messaged and talked on the phone non-stop. She wasn't in my class since she was a senior, but she did go to my school. That should have provided a great opportunity for sideways glances in the hallways and cute winks and hellos after class. Except for one thing.

She was a twin.

I couldn't for the life of me tell her and her sister apart. I'd see a familiar face walking toward me in the hallway and I'd panic.

Was it her? Or her sister? Just trying to play it cool and be nice to one girl is enough for a teenage boy. Trying to navigate sisters has proven to be difficult for even the most seasoned of men. The idea of flirting with the wrong sister and the repercussions that would undoubtedly follow left me paralyzed. So I came up with the most brilliant strategy that my puberty stricken brain could muster. I ignored her until she spoke first. If she did, I'd take a quick mental note of her outfit and log it into my memory.

"Jeans, red hoodie. That's your girl. Jeans, graphic tee-shirt, not your girl."

That would buy me a day of being able to tell her apart from her sister. And it seemed like a good system to me until I got a message on my phone.

"I'm starting to think you don't like me. Are you just too good for me, Zak?"

"What? Why the hell would you say that?" I texted back.

"I saw you today in the hallway and you didn't even say hi."

I wasn't sure if it was worse to act like I hadn't noticed her or to break it to her that I couldn't tell her and her sister apart. I vowed to do better. And it worked. Slowly, I learned to tell the small differences between her and her sister. We texted constantly. After several weeks, I invited her to hang out at my house over the weekend and she said yes. I was usually awkward around girls and groups of people but with her it was easy. We fell into effortless conversation.

I loved the smile on her face and the way she laughed. Most of all, I loved how I felt when I was with her. I felt like myself. No mask, no persona, no trying to be anyone but The Real Zak.

She became a permanent fixture in my life. Most weekends were spent at my house, talking, cuddling, watching movies, and making out. We never went to her house and only went out for a movie a handful of times. Maybe it should have bothered me that she never really seemed to want to show off our relationship, but I was too happy and too taken with her to care.

Over the following months, she became my world. I bought her flowers, I wrote her notes, I even told her I loved her. And I did. I cared for her as deeply as my fifteen-year-old heart could. I felt happy, secure, content, and myself. I felt like I belonged. And that was a first for me. I had never bonded or connected easily with others and I drank in the euphoria that comes from acceptance.

That year I bought new clothes and made it my goal to dress impeccably. I looked like the preppy cover boy for American Eagle. I didn't smoke or drink much because she didn't. She wasn't interested in alcohol. So naturally, I wasn't either. I didn't hang out with my friends as often as I had before. Spending every waking hour with her was all I wanted to do. People made fun of me for my clothes. They called me a fag and whispered that I was gay. And while that might have wrecked me just a few months before, I let it slide easily off my back, knowing that I had her approval.

After several months, I heard rumors that she was texting and spending time at another guy's house. That ate at me. I felt jealous. Insecure. Fearful. One night, I recruited a buddy of mine to ride with me as I followed her to see where she was going. Real *Bourne Identity* kind of shit. She parked at another guy's house. Anger rose up. Then it turned to rage. We waited until she came out - me raking my hands through my hair, fuming and cursing the whole time. She made us right away. We ducked our heads down like a couple of dumb cops on a stakeout and tried to get away, but she was already furious.

You can guess what kind of fight I had on my hands after a stunt like that. It took us days to reconnect. I was so desperate to have her back, so afraid I'd lose her, that I just apologized. I didn't even ask where she was or what she was doing. I didn't want to think about it. I just wanted to feel happy and see her smile again. And I got what I wanted.

For a little while.

As she approached graduation and prepared to head off for college, I could feel her growing distant. I wouldn't have admitted it to anyone, even myself at the time, but I couldn't shake the nagging feeling that something was off between us. I pushed in harder, thinking that maybe if I tried more, messaged more, or said more that gap would close. I came in like a tidal wave, fueled by the fear of losing her.

Then one day I got a text that read:

"Zak, I need to tell you something. You know I'm leaving for college and I just wanted to let you know that I am going to start dating another guy."

My heart crashed to the floor. All the feelings of inferiority, rejection, and insecurity bubbled to the surface. I didn't really have anyone but her. I wanted her, I needed her.

"But what about us?"

I sat waiting for her reply.

But I wasn't prepared for the text that followed.

"It was just a fun time, Zak."

Those few words shattered me into a million pieces. Was I just a fun time? That's all I was worth? My mind flooded with memories and I scoured them for proof that I hadn't been wrong all along, that she felt as deeply for me as I did for her, that she actually cared about me. Was I once again the one who didn't really belong? The kid with the cash beside the pool, the guy with the flowers and a house to hang out at?

I felt duped. Alone. Rejected. And angry.

In hindsight, my naiveté is obvious. She was a good girl and became a smart, beautiful, successful woman who I still know and keep in touch with today. But I was the classic teenaged boy who couldn't take a hint, couldn't read between the lines and who listened to every piece of gossip his friends told him, who overreacted, who came on too strong. We were young. We were still playing at love and life. And she knew that. But I didn't.

I gave her everything.

And it broke my heart.

After that, nothing seemed to matter. It was as if all the color had drained out of life. I told myself that maybe there was no such thing as real connection, no such thing as people who actually liked other people simply for who they were, not for what they could get in return. If the one person that I had actually showed my truest self to didn't accept me and tossed me out like a disposable napkin, then who would?

I was invited to the sixteenth birthday party of one of my classmates not long after and I decided to go. I milled between the little huddles of teenagers, carrying my plastic cup filled with soda, the drink of choice for the night. There was a DJ and everyone seemed ready to have a good time. I needed to blow off some steam. I tried to focus on the beat of the music and forget all thoughts of Abbey.

Before I knew it, I was in the midst of a dance circle, fueled by happy teenage hormones and a little caffeine buzz from soda. Everyone laughed and showed off their best dance moves. I heard someone shout for me to smile for a picture and I draped my arms around the friends closest to me. The flash of that camera froze a moment in time. A moment of innocence and happiness that would never return after that night.

After the camera clicked, I felt a tap on my shoulder.

"Hey, let's get out of here," one of my friends whispered in my ear.

"Go where?"

"We got invited to another party. Should be a good time." The way he grinned told me that the party we were going to next wasn't going to be serving soda and pretzels.

"Let's go," I said.

We didn't want to show up empty handed so we put our heads together and figured out a way to obtain a half gallon jug of Vladimir vodka. We might as well have brought rubbing alcohol to the party, but we didn't know any better. Alcohol was alcohol to us and we felt proud to have obtained some of our very own.

As I approached the house, I felt nervous. I could hear the heavy base of the music inside and it matched the pounding of my own heart. I tried to act cool as I slipped in the door, quickly realizing that my friend and I were, without a doubt, the youngest people there. Everyone looked to be about my brother's age. I told myself that I was growing up, getting older. It was about time I began to close the seven-year gap between us. I grabbed a plastic cup and filled it liberally with Gatorade and vodka. I drank it as fast as I could, hoping that it would relax me as it slid down my throat.

I tried to blend in, smiling with the others, laughing loudly at the punchline of jokes. I watched as smoke curled from the cigarettes of a group of guys in the corner. They were the legends, the ones that we all looked up to, wanted to be.

Movement by the door caught my eye and I looked up to see my brother stepping into the room.

He caught eyes with me immediately.

"What the fuck is he doing here?"

He was angry.

Not so much with me but with whoever had brought me. Everyone shrugged and passed blame under their breath as the beat of the music wore on. Everyone knew better than to upset my brother. If the guys in that room were legends, he was the king. But he seemed to know something I didn't, a darker side to that life I idolized. He wanted to protect me. But I stayed.

Once the clock passed midnight, time slowed into a blur. I remember snapshots of it, like impressions of a dream. My brother leaving, muttering something under his breath about the party being lame. The burning feeling of alcohol as I pounded back drink after drink. An older girl pressing her body close to me. An uncomfortable feeling spreading over me as her touch grew more intentional and direct.

I was a virgin and I was nervous. Sure, I talked to my friends as if I was confident, experienced, and sexually mature. But inside I was shy, nervous, and unsure of myself.

The more furious her advances became, the more resistant I felt. Even beneath the fog of alcohol, I knew I didn't have feelings for her, not like I had with Abbey. I didn't want to cross the line. Not here. Not in that way.

And then suddenly, I jerked awake. My body felt thick and groggy. I looked around. I was on a couch and my head was pounding. I blinked and tried to remember what had happened the night before. I stood and slowly made my way to the bathroom as if wearing lead boots.

Once inside, I shut the door. I stood in front of the mirror for a moment as the fog dissipated just enough to begin to grasp at memories from the hours prior. And then, strange markings on my shoulders caught my eye. I turned and faced my bare back toward the mirror. Scratch marks covered my back.

I wasn't a virgin anymore.

I stood there for a moment and my stomach turned. I felt cheap.

Used.

Worthless.

Disposable.

It was my first sexual experience and it was terrible. It wasn't special or meaningful. It was empty and void of love. Most people think teenage boys are just horny creatures without feeling, happy to fuck anything willing.

But that's not always the case. At least not at first.

I stood there, recalling the uncomfortable night. I remembered asking her to move away from me as she fell asleep just because I couldn't bear to feel the sensation of her skin on mine anymore.

So this is it, I thought.

Suddenly, I was that little boy beside the pool giving away my money, hoping for the chance at being accepted.

This is what it's like to live in the real world. You get your heart broken, your virginity stolen, you feel discarded and thrown away.

Suddenly, my sadness turned to resolution.

This is life.

These are the players.

This is the game.

And so I played.

From that moment on, I accepted every invitation to every party I could find. I drowned my social anxieties in alcohol and marijuana, hoping that somehow that shy, hurting boy inside me would fade away.

And he did.

With each drink and pill I popped, I became stronger, louder, funnier, sexier, and braver.

If there was a dance circle, I was in the middle of it. If there was a dare, I was the first to take it. With enough liquor, I didn't feel my anxiety. Now, instead of being the kid on the sidelines, I was in the middle. I had the power. I found myself making fun of others, enjoying the fact that it was now me who was saying the cutting one-liners, humiliating someone else in the same way I had been humiliated so many times before. And isn't that how it often goes? The bullied kid becomes the bully? People called me crazy, called me a dick. But I preferred being the dick who was the life of the party, who made everyone laugh instead of the outcast on the sidelines.

"Z-MAN! Z-MAN! Z-MAN!" they would chant.

The Real Zak was nervous and shy. The Real Zak could be hurt.

But not Z-Man.

Z-Man would dance without feeling nervous and have sex with any girl who was willing without any trace of insecurity.

Z-Man made friends.

Z-Man was brave.

Z-Man was invincible.

Chapter 4: Blow

With Z-Man in the picture, my life became a steady rhythm. Go to school, play sports, head into the weekend with the goal of downing as much alcohol and banging as many girls as I could. Our small town didn't offer much else to do. This was actually considered a fairly acceptable lifestyle. Even the majority of the adults in Millersburg still beat to this same rhythm, just in their own way. Maybe they weren't going to parties and having sex with strangers, but most still lived for Friday night when the drinking could fully commence.

Work hard, play hard.

This was the way of the working class folk of our town.

One weekend my parents went out of town and word got around that I would be alone at my house. Within no time, a group of seniors approached me, all smiles.

"Z-Man!" they shouted.

"We're going to have a party up in the mountains this weekend and we'd love for you to come."

I smiled eagerly. "Just tell me where to go."

"Well, see, that's the thing. The place we have picked out in the mountains is just so far. It will be such a pain in the ass for everyone to drive there. It would be so much better if we could do it somewhere closer."

There was a pause and I could feel what was going to come next.

"Word is that your folks are going to be out of town this weekend which means your house will be free. Any chance we could throw the party there?"

I felt like the kid at the edge of the pool with the pocket full of cash again. The Real Zak felt butterflies at the idea of that many people coming to *my* house and the burden of keeping a secret from my parents. But Z-Man had to say yes.

And Z-Man always won out.

It was a Friday and the party was scheduled for that evening. My stomach twisted and turned in knots in the hours leading up to the it. My parents wanted me to stay with my grandmother while they were away and I worked to get out of it without attracting suspicion, something about how I preferred to sleep in my own bed and being old enough to stay on my own.

As the hours counted down, I felt panicked. The closer it got, the jumpier and more nervous I felt. I needed The Real Zak to shut up and let Z-Man take over. He was tough. Capable. Cunning. Confident. But I knew all too well that Z-Man wasn't going to show until I started smoking and drinking.

With the panic mounting, I heard the sound of vehicles.. We had agreed that everyone would come to my house by a back property entrance, through a big field, so as not to attract attention. A group of older guys pulled up first and started unloading their vehicles. Out came drinks, snacks, and speakers - everything needed to throw a party. I quickly realized that I wasn't as in charge as I would have liked to think. I felt like a bystander, a guest in my own house as they moved about. Moving things, directing people as if they were the ones hosting the party. I stood in the corner, unsure of what to say, heart racing and palms sweating.

I only hoped for points in the game we were all playing at - the game of buying and selling acceptance. Surely throwing a kegger at sixteen-years-old would earn me some respect.

Anxiety gripped me, but I told myself it would be gone soon. I knew how to numb it, how to get my fears and inhibitions to subside. It was almost time. Almost time to start drinking. And then Z-Man would take things from there.

The moment I saw someone start pouring a drink, I generously filled a glass and downed it.

And filled another. And another.

It was taking more than it used to for Z-Man to come out.

Someone offered me weed and I took it gratefully.

Finally, by midnight, Z-Man had emerged.

No more panic, no more inhibitions. I felt brave. Free from my anxious, racing thoughts, free from my social fears.

After a while, my friend and I made our way to my room to smoke more weed. We watched the movie *Grandma's Boy* on repeat. We laughed uncontrollably. We lay there and threw quarters at the stucco wall, listening to the interesting noise it made. We kept throwing, making dents in the soft stucco. I lay there, without a care. I didn't know who was milling about my home or hooking up in the kitchen or living room. It hardly felt like my house anymore and I didn't care.

My head buzzed and my vision blurred but still, I didn't care. That was the beautiful part of it, *I didn't care about anything.*

I spent much of the next day cleaning before my parents got home. A few people offered to help me, but the majority stumbled and snuck home without another thought. Oddly, I didn't resent the cleanup duty. My head hurt a little and I felt foggy but I felt proud of myself for pulling it off. I had earned the points I so desperately wanted. Maybe I was finally accepted after all.

Everyone likes Z-Man, I told myself.

For so long, I had tried to be so many things. I pretended to be every character from every movie. I tried every style of clothing. I tried to fit in, tried to earn myself a seat at the table. And it seemed that I had finally found the door, the entrance, the character.

Z-Man.

Everyone likes Z-Man.

My parents didn't catch me that time, but a few months later they did. My friend and I had agreed to use each other as an alibi when our parents asked us where we were going for the night. We would tell them that we were staying at the other one's house. For months, our parents took our word for it, never double checking the story. But then one night, after a lot of alcohol, a series of unfortunate events took place that involved us hitting a stop sign and getting a flat tire, we were forced to call our parents. They were not happy when they showed up to assess the situation. But that was nothing compared to the look on their faces when they began to compare notes with the other parents and the realization began to sink in that they had been lied to for months. I still remember the look on my mom's face as she spoke to my friend's mom, that sadness in her eyes. The loss of trust.

"Zak, I'm so disappointed in you," she said.

I hated it. I hated disappointing her. I wanted to assure her that it wouldn't happen again, but deep down inside I knew that I couldn't. I couldn't let go of Z-Man. I needed him now. He was my ticket. My entrance into acceptance and belonging. Is there any currency more valuable? Anything more powerful?

I tried for a while. Tried to forget Z-Man. Tried not to drink or experiment with drugs.

But a few months later, in between classes at school, a friend of mine motioned me over in his direction.

"I got something for you."

"What is it?" I asked.

"It's Seroquel. It's an antipsychotic or some shit. Just take half of this pill and then try to stay awake. Trust me." He smiled like I was in for the treat of my life.

So I popped the entire pill into my mouth and headed into first period.

"If I start falling asleep, wake me up," I whispered to the kid in front of me just before class started.

He nodded dutifully.

As class began, a wave of sleepiness swept over me. I felt a kick in my shins.

"Zak, wake up," he hissed.

I jerked and sat up, but that tidal wave of sleepiness wouldn't dissipate. Raising eyelids felt like lifting a boulder. Trying to keep them open was almost pointless.

Finally, class was dismissed. I stood up. And then the world morphed into a new place that I had never been. There were voices. There were faces. I began to walk the halls and the sounds that filled them sounded both far away and simultaneously amplified.

"Hey, Z-Man!"

"What's up, Z-Man?"

I couldn't answer. I wanted to get away. I wanted the noise to stop.

I covered my ears and took off running - straight down the hallway, up two flights of stairs, and past the gym. Between the lunchroom and band room, there was an indention in the wall with a set of doors. I slumped into the cubby, laid back, and covered my eyes.

I am so fucked up.

I forced myself to open my eyes and I looked at the lockers above me. Bright colors swirled through my vision, bursting and snaking through the drab lockers.

Zak, you have to get help. You are not okay.

I knew the nurse's station was just down the hall. Even without looking in the mirror, I knew my face was whiter than snow. Faces stared at me as I walked toward the nurse's station. The trek felt like miles.

The nurse turned and looked in my direction as I entered the room.

"Headache. Sleep. Now."

It was all I could manage to say. I fell onto the cot in the corner of the room and released my body into the sleep it so desperately craved.

When I came to, her fingers were on my wrist. She pulled her hand back and looked me over, obviously worried by how slow my pulse was.

"Did you take something you shouldn't have?" she asked.

"No, no, no," I lied. "I just want to go to sleep."

A while later, my mom arrived at the school to pick me up. I stood up and walked down the halls toward her vehicle. I passed a friend of mine and he looked at me knowingly. I knew I was never going to live this day down.

"The nurse said she thought you might be on drugs." My mom looked at me as if she was suggesting something outlandish.

"No, no, no, I would never do that," I jumped in quickly.

She looked relieved. "No, of course not. I didn't really think so. I just wanted to ask."

My mom called the local health center to try and get me in to see a doctor, but there weren't any openings for another few hours. I fell into another deep sleep as we waited. When I awoke, I felt groggy but the hallucinations had cleared and there were no longer any notable symptoms or signs for the doctors to see.

I rehearsed my cover story about how I mixed my acid reflux pills accidentally with something else and peddled it to the doctors when they came into my room for an examination. Somehow, they bought the bullshit. Or perhaps they didn't care enough to challenge it.

I decided to push my luck.

"You know, I feel like I should mention that I do have a lot of trouble going to sleep," I spoke up. "It's just so hard, you know, trying to get into a good, deep sleep and then stay asleep. Is there anything that would help with that?"

I left that day with a prescription for Ambien.

The irony is as rich as it is sad, the fact that I went into a medical center because I had overdosed on a medication provided by a fellow high school student and left with a prescription of my own. It was almost too easy.

My mom didn't say anything but she held onto the prescription and refused to fill it.

"You don't need this, Zak. This stuff is bad, I promise."

On the second account, she was right. The drugs were bad for me.

But on the first account, she was wrong, at least from my point of view.

I did need them. Maybe not Seroquel, maybe not something every day. But I needed my superpower, I needed substances that made Z-Man come out. Z-Man was who everyone knew and liked. Z-Man was the one who bought drinks and made friends. Letting him go was unthinkable.

Though parties are what I remember most about those years, I also played sports. I made the basketball team and we did well. Our small-town team even made the playoffs. I was benched for a large portion of the season but on the night of the district championship game, I felt a tap on my shoulder.

"You're in," the coach said.

"What?" I wasn't sure I'd heard correctly.

I turned to my buddy, "What the fuck did he just say?"

"He said 'you're in!'"

"Get in there!" he yelled. I stood up and my legs felt weak and shaky. I always felt anxiety when people looked at me.

The stands were packed. With all those eyes and all those faces I felt tunnel-visioned and my stomach tied itself in knots. I was no stranger to this feeling. It had followed me constantly throughout my years of playing sports. There were no substances to calm me, no drinks to bring out the brave and uninhibited Z-Man.

Nobody but The Real Zak.

I walked over to the check-in table and I could hardly stand. My legs shook uncontrollably.

C'mon Zak. Get it together.

The game began and I gave it everything I had. I played my heart out, better than I had all season. But when a foul was called and the game paused for a moment I realized that my anxiety had left my mouth dry and my lips immobilized. They were curled all the way up around my gums, exposing my teeth. I looked crazy.

But despite the flood of anxiety, I battled to play on the field that day. It was a victory, not because we won, which we didn't, but because I got out there and performed well. It was all me, all Zak. Those memories were good ones. Memories of life unattached to substances or alcohol. Memories when I still felt like I had control. Memories of a time when partying, drinking, and doing drugs were only a thread, before addiction became woven into the very fabric of my being.

I played basketball from ninth through twelfth grade, and I believe that more of my truest self was revealed on that court than anywhere else during those years. I felt motivated and clear-headed. My jaded and tough exterior dropped and I was kind to my fellow players, doing anything I could to pull the team together. When it was time to huddle up, I'd nudge the younger, more timid players to stand in front of me. In twelfth grade, I was point guard. When we'd form a line, the less experienced players would stand back, assuming that I'd be at the front of the line. But I'd shake my head and encourage them to stand ahead of me. I knew what it was like to feel like the odd man out, the misfit, the extra. I wanted them to feel like part of the group, accepted, and appreciated. On those courts, The Real Zak emerged and stood tall and strong.

But that didn't mean that Z-Man stayed away. Despite these glimpses of goodness, I still struggled with constant social anxiety. With each passing year, the pressure to drink up and party hard grew stronger and stronger. I wanted to be liked and accepted. Drinking and partying was just what everyone did. But after a while, the newness of alcohol and popping a few pills wasn't enough.

One night, I sat in a car with a group of friends outside the bowling alley and movement from the front seat caught my eye.

"Whatcha got?" I asked, trying to make out what the guy in the passenger seat was holding.

"Don't you dare give him any. His brother will fucking kill us," the other guy in the driver's seat said harshly, shooting him a look of warning.

"C'mon, I want to see. Don't worry about my big brother," I begged.

The guy with the item gave me a long look.

"Follow me," he said.

He led the way into the bowling alley building. It was a small establishment with only a few lanes, a concession stand, and a bar. He turned and walked down a narrow, dimly lit hallway and then through the doors of the tiny men's bathroom. Thin, peeling walls created a single stall and he opened it for me. I stepped past the urinal, crusted in dried piss, and joined him.

We stood uncomfortably close to one another, me waiting for what was coming next. I assumed he would give me a couple of pills to pop.

Instead, he pulled a small clear bag from his wallet, secured by a blue twisty-tie. He opened the bag and slid his credit card in, retrieving a small amount.

"What is this?" I asked.

"Just do it," he prompted, holding it toward me.

I placed my index finger on my right nostril and bent down until I could feel the plastic brush against my skin. I inhaled sharply, sucking the powder into my nose. In that split second, I knew that whatever I had just snorted was not anything I had ever snorted before. I felt a dripping sensation in the back of my throat and an earthy taste spread through my mouth. Then suddenly, my tongue, nose, and throat went numb.

He followed suit and grinned at me.

"You just snorted coke, my friend."

He slapped my back with a grin and opened the latch of the stall, leading the way back into the bowling alley. I followed, feeling proud and accomplished. I had just done cocaine for the first time. Scenes from *Scarface* flashed through my mind as I threw my shoulders back with a new buzz of confidence and rejoined my friends. I was a real man now. Like my brother.

And just like that, Z-Man had a whole new set of superpowers.

Looking back, it's easy to see the beginnings of toxic habits in my life. It's easy to see the darkness. That's what everyone focuses on when you're talking about addiction. But few people talk about the fact that it's not all bad in the beginning. It's not all darkness. No one wakes up one day and decides to become an addict. Few even realize that it's happening until it's too late. You're just the kid grabbing candy from the shelf and eating it without buying it.

Those who lower their nose to the pile of powder or get drunk aren't always immediate addicts. Sometimes it's just a curious teenager who wants to feel tough and empowered. Or a kid riddled with anxiety who just wants to talk to girls. Or the one who just wants to be liked and doesn't feel that they bring enough life to the party all on their own.

I have good memories of that time, if I'm being honest. Memories of meeting people, talking, laughing, feeling liberated from my anxiety, and feeling on top of the world. We were still young and still full of hope and promise then. We were the future business owners, future parents, artists, and engineers.

We had the whole world in front of us.

We were free.

Or at least that's what we thought.

Chapter 5: Missing the Train

Have you ever noticed how many movies take place in New York, Chicago, or California? Opening credits are set to images of skyscrapers, panoramic shots of people flooding New York intersections, or sunny California beaches dotted with sprawling houses. For the expansive land we call our country, these relatively small areas occupy the spotlight. But it's not really odd when you think about it. These places are iconic, exciting, and sexy. They have become what America is best known for.

But what if movies were shot in the backdrop of the space in between? The space where countless families work, live, and raise their children? What would you see then?

You'd likely see an area that resembles the one I grew up in. You'd see a small town with a couple of cheap grocery stores, a handful of pizza shops, a bowling alley, a drive-in theater, a school, a few churches, and bars.

Though many technological advancements have been made and changes have taken place in these towns, they are, in many ways, very reminiscent of what they were a hundred years ago. And people still live their lives in much the same way. You go to school, maybe college, you find something you're decent at and start work as soon as possible. You meet a nice boy or girl and you get married. You buy a house and have a few kids. You retire if you can and watch your kids repeat much of the same cycle. The path is simple and well-worn from all those who have followed it. You work hard during the week and count down the days until Friday. For fun, you bowl, watch a movie at the drive-in theater, go to the bar, catch the local sports game, or go to church. There isn't much that's new or different. You can pretty much guess what your entire life is going to look like as a child. You can only hope you find a career you really love or meet a woman who takes your breath away because everything else is fairly predictable.

Until you get drunk. Until you pop pills. Until you lean in and snort a little pile of white powder.

And suddenly, everything changes. A shock of stimulation runs through you that you've never experienced before. You feel like you can do anything. Suddenly, laughing at the antics of the same friends you've had since kindergarten is a thrill. Suddenly the drive-in movie is hilarious. Suddenly, feeling the throb of music pulsing through your body feels like the pinnacle of life. Your small world explodes into a kaleidoscope of colors you've never seen.

And it's hard to ever want to see it the other way again.

A whole new world opened up to me when I realized how many options were available to create new experiences in my unchanging environment. Alcohol made me feel one way. This pill made me feel another. These pills made me feel something else entirely. Together, the combination created its own, unique experience.

I knew what it felt like to eat pizza in the little pizza shop. I knew what it felt like to go to school. I knew what it felt like to listen to music and dance. I knew what it felt like to see a movie.

But with the discovery of drugs and alcohol, everything changed. I could create a whole new universe, a whole new world of existence unlike anything I had ever felt before. And I wasn't the only one. Drug and alcohol use were rampant among kids from sixteen to twenty-five-years-old in Millersburg. And I'm not even so sure it stopped then. I think marriage, jobs, and families simply forced extreme habits to morph into a version more accepted by society - sending the 8-to-5er to blow off steam at a bar on a Friday, the businessman to snort a little coke, and the mom to pour herself a third glass of wine when the kids are asleep.

Because once you experience life through the colored glasses of substance, you don't want to go back. Or at least that was the case for me. Alcohol and substances were my means of turning into a different version of myself. A version of myself who seemed to have a much easier time in life than The Real Zak did. With enough sips and swallowed pills, my constant nervousness would go away, my racing mind would grow numb, and my paralyzing social anxiety would dissolve. And so, with the power to alter both myself and my perceptions of the small world I lived within, the choice to drink and do drugs seemed like a no brainer.

Even at seventeen, eighteen, and nineteen years old, obtaining drugs and hard liquor was easy. In small towns, the demand and supply are both high. In the early days, I indulged mostly on the weekends when I didn't have school and work. I went to any party I was invited to and I accepted invitations to hang out at friends' houses as often as possible. As soon as I arrived, I inhaled and swallowed away my shyness and anxiety so that a more confident version of myself, along with a whole world of technicolor, could emerge. It was an upgrade. An upgrade of me and an upgrade of the unchanging small town around me.

I remember my friends piling into the bed of my truck and hunching down while I pulled a tarp over top. We would sneak into the drive-in theater without paying a cent. We'd drink, swallow, and snort anything we could find until the drive-in movie slid behind the filtered lens of substance and the whole world seemed different. Every so often, we'd get a tap on the window as we sat there watching, someone would offer us whatever was available that night, and we handed out fistfuls of money for bags filled with pills. Half the time, we didn't even know what we were taking. We snorted ten capsules each of some substance and grew angry when it did nothing to alter us. We found out later that we had been sold a bag of some kind of medication without any cool side effects to speak of.

I was pretty good at hiding my newfound habits. But halfway through eleventh grade, my parents caught me. Nowhere to hide, no way to spin the story, they saw me in all my drunken glory. I don't even remember how it happened to be honest, because those months and memories are all a blur, somewhere in the haze that drugs and alcohol create. That night, all I remember is that everything seemed to swirl. I remember crying. I remember seeing the look of sadness on their faces. They didn't ground me or take away all my privileges. They simply looked at me and said, "Zak, we are so disappointed in you."

That hit me to my core. More than anything, I wanted to be loved and accepted. The idea of disappointing someone I cared about hurt worse than any measure of discipline they could have doled out. The distance and strain it created between us felt like rejection and that hit me hard. The next day, I vowed to find a way to live my life without drugs and alcohol.

I was successful for quite a few months. I didn't drink, I didn't do drugs. It felt good, living life entirely as The Real Zak - something I hadn't done since I was a kid. But I soon found myself missing the way the world looked under the influence of substances. I missed the crazy, brave Z-Man who everyone seemed to love. I missed the ability to drink until my senses dulled and my mind quieted.

One night I gave in. *Just one drink,* I told myself. But then I had another. My body buzzed with warmth. And then I remembered. I remembered the way it felt to be Z-Man. To feel invulnerable and confident. To feel so invested in the present moment that everything else just fades away. I didn't necessarily feel happy, but I did feel euphoric - like floating above the world in apathetic bliss.

I told myself I wouldn't keep drinking and partying. I reminded myself of the sad eyes and disappointed faces of my parents. But I couldn't say no to the party invitations that came my way and I couldn't pass up the chance to feel like the invincible Z-Man for a while. I found myself sliding back into old patterns and habits: work hard during the week, play hard on the weekends.

As time moved on, however, I needed Z-Man and that world of numbness more and more often. I felt bored at school, took little fulfillment in my job, and had no idea what my purpose in life was and who I might be outside this little world. Even sports held little excitement as I watched the baseball team I signed up to play with fail miserably game after game. And game after game, I traced my toe through the sand in the outfield thinking, *Is this really all life has to offer? Is this my forever world? This tiny Millersburg universe?*

I hated the thought of it.

One day, I poured out half of my large jug of red Gatorade and filled it to the brim with vodka and brought it on the field with me. I gulped down the first few mouthfuls with urgency, awaiting the transportation from my world into an alternate version of it, where edges and lines smeared into blissful apathy.

I offered my jug to a friend of mine beside me, "Want some Gatorade?" I asked with a knowing smile.

He grabbed it and took a generous swig and promptly spewed it onto the ground.

"What the fuck is that?" he asked, his face still puckered.

"It's vodka," I said laughing uncontrollably.

He didn't want to join me in my version of a baseball game and that was alright with me. I kept drinking. Soon my body felt heavy and the landscape blurred as I sat, waiting for the game to be over.

Suddenly I wasn't even sure why I was there, why I was forcing myself to sit and participate on a team that sucked as much as we did. The Real Zak wanted to please, to be a part of the team even if losing was in the cards every game. But Z-Man was the one on the field now. And he didn't give two flying fucks about sports.

I felt my legs stand and heard my voice echo as if I was in a dream.

"I'm done," I said, looking at my coach.

"Okay, I'll give you a little break and put somebody in the rotation before you," he said, not understanding.

"No, I'm DONE," I said more emphatically. Z-Man knew exactly what he wanted.

My coach followed me and begged me not to leave. I was one of the better players, even while drunk. The Real Zak would have felt anxious and apologetic, meeting eyes with the coach. But Z-Man didn't waver.

I walked to my truck, hopped in the driver's side, turned the key, drove home and went straight to bed, sleeping off my drunken state.

A few months later, a group of friends invited me to an underage dance club. It promised all the music and fun without the alcohol typically associated with clubs. I loved to dance and I agreed. The music thumped away and I found myself lost in it. My body moved, even without alcohol greasing my veins and it felt good. I could see and feel everything around me with such perfect clarity and I loved it. Dead sober, I held nothing back, my body pulsing to the beat. That was a first, being free without the influence of alcohol and drugs.

And I met a girl that night.

She was sweet and said she liked my dancing. We talked for a while and exchanged phone numbers. In no time, we were texting constantly and went out together soon after. She was one of the few people who didn't know me as Z-Man. She has seen The Real Zak on that dance floor. That felt good. She grew quickly attached to me. I liked her and enjoyed the acceptance I felt when I was with her. She added color and fun to my real world. Suddenly, I found myself with less of a desire to party.

"You know, you're really not such a douchebag," she said to me one day.

"What do you mean?" I asked with a laugh.

"I mean, you're known for being so macho and confident. You're known as the crazy guy at parties. But you're actually a good guy. And you kind of have a sweet side."

Her words made me happy but uncomfortable. It felt good to be seen and accepted, to have the love of a girl. But the idea that someone could see and touch The Real Zak was terrifying. I reminded myself what had happened the last time I allowed myself to care deeply for someone and my true nature to be seen. My heart was broken. I couldn't let that happen again.

That fear of rejection caused me to be paranoid constantly. My eyes and ears were always open, looking for any sign or clue that she wasn't faithful, that she was betraying me. Most of the time, I hid my skeptical eyes well. But when we went to parties together and I began to drink, Z-Man would emerge and it was a whole different story. I would grow loud and angry at the sight of her talking to other people. I'd intrude upon her conversations, cutting in with rude comments and hateful faces.

This dynamic between us made for a very tumultuous relationship. We would be together one minute and break up the next. We'd each retaliate when broken up by seeing other people, which only planted more seeds of distrust when we'd get back together. Sometimes, she could see me, *the real me,* and it felt good. During those times, I had small tastes of a life worth living outside of alcohol and drugs. But my fear of rejection quickly overshadowed those glimpses and paranoia plagued me. Each time we broke up, I partied harder, throwing all caution to the wind and pushing my body to the limits of how drunk or strung out it was capable of getting.

And so my junior and senior years of high school are filed away in my mind, not as a series of chronological memories, but rather a blurred recollection of scattered moments - like the shapes and visions that come back to you after dreaming, prompting the feeling of a memory without a full understanding of it. And though I couldn't have told you at the time, I think that's exactly what I wanted. I wanted the edges of my days and weeks to blur together because I couldn't bear to live them in real time. My life consisted of the same cycle - me surviving the hours of school and work for the promise of escape by nights and weekends. I lived for that first sip.

The prospect of the decades ahead of me that would likely follow this same pattern in more grown-up form caused a gnawing feeling of unrest inside. It pushed me to greater extremes with each week and party that passed.

The closer I drew to graduation, the more that feeling gnawed at me. I knew the expected path ahead. Go to college, get a job and work hard, marry a nice girl, and have kids. Most people around me seemed perfectly content with that idea. I couldn't get away from the feeling that I was meant for more. What that was, I had no idea. So I tried to push any thought of the future from my mind. I didn't know what career I wanted to pursue. I didn't know any girls who I'd actually like to spend my life with. And I was deathly afraid that I would be the one person who couldn't fold into the cookie cutter that everyone else seemed to. What if I failed? What if I didn't meet the right girl? What if no one wanted to marry me?

I looked for anything that would give me a plan for my future. Once, I considered starting my own pizza shop. I had worked at a pizza shop before and it was something I knew how to do. I also knew that I could follow in my dad's footsteps in the family business, which was wildly successful. I knew my mom wanted me to go to college.

People underestimate the pressure that is placed on young adults at that pivotal transition period between graduating high school and whatever comes next. It feels like the whole world is looking at you expectantly, waiting for you to make a final decision on the course of your life. The pressure is crushing. My world was so small and the only path I could imagine for myself was the same one that everyone around me had chosen. But I didn't *want* it. I felt defeated, like the one person in the room who didn't receive the same memo on how to proceed, the one person deathly afraid of the future. No one else asked questions, no one challenged the status quo. Everyone just went about trying to get into college and pursuing romantic relationships. I couldn't find joy in either.

The Real Zak was shy, insecure, and unsure about the future. I needed Z-Man, the brave, undaunted version of myself. I needed that larger than life feeling because the idea of my life and future was swallowing me whole. And so I drank before my SAT exam in hopes that I would feel gutsy and strong, or at the very least, unconcerned with the results.

Senior week came and my whole class planned a trip to Ocean City, Maryland. We bought cases of beer and I partied like my life depended on it as soon as I arrived. I just wanted to make those days and nights last as long as possible - free from the worry of what was ahead, of what my test scores would be.

My fears mounted. The idea of going to college, of facing a whole sea of unfamiliar faces induced paralyzing anxiety inside of me. So I drank and then drank more. I popped pills and then popped more. Anything to push the future as far away as possible.

But I couldn't put it off forever.

As it turned out, I scored terribly on the SAT test. Z-Man wasn't the giant and hero in the test room that he was on the dance floor.

Even still, it was time to make choices on my next steps.

From the outside, I probably just looked like an irresponsible teenager, wasting time away. But I was scared and lost. It was easier to sink into the oblivion that drugs and alcohol created than to deal with the fact that I couldn't find any sense of direction or purpose to my life.

The more I looked around at others, the more I felt out of place. Everyone else had picked colleges and careers and had serious relationships. Everyone talked about what they wanted to study and where they wanted to go to college. They were excited, expectant. I was terrified because I had no clue what I wanted to do.

After high school, life feels like a train picking up speed down the tracks. At first, there's plenty of time to hop on and gain momentum, but the faster it gets, the harder it becomes to make the jump. You see your friends making the jump, taking jobs, marrying girls, looking happy and content to ride off into life. You keep telling yourself that the next car is the one you're going to hop on, but you keep missing the jump. And suddenly, the fear of being the only person not on the train, the only person left behind, the only person who didn't figure out how to follow the expected path, grips you until you can't breathe.

People expect you to hop on the train. People always ask you what you're going to be, what you're going to do with your life. But rarely do people ask you if you even *want* to be on the train; rarely do they ask what fulfills you or makes you happy.

All around me, I saw people who had jumped and let life take them down the tracks. They worked mid-level jobs that paid enough to get by, they had a few kids, they took a few trips, and then they retired. It all seemed pointless to me, so sad and unfulfilling.

I wanted more. But as quickly as hope or desire would spark, it would extinguish in a flood of self-hatred. Who was I to dream big or think that I could achieve big things in life? Wasn't I just Zak, a small-town kid who would probably always live in a small-town world? I didn't deserve anything more, so why should I even try?

On the outside, I appeared to be nothing but washed-up. A deadbeat. A kid who didn't care about anything. But quite the opposite was true. It was actually my desire for a life with meaning that rendered the expected path unfulfilling. It was my inability to conform that left me feeling defeated. I didn't know how to accept the idea of spending my life on a track that wasn't fueled by a sense of personal fulfillment. I didn't know how to pretend that I liked the life that everyone else seemed to like. And so I drank. I did drugs. I popped pills. The closer and closer I got to graduation, the more I did. The only thing I knew how to do was push tomorrow as far away as possible.

Sometimes addicts begin not as deadbeats and washouts, but simply as those honest enough to admit that they aren't happy and fulfilled and are too scared to do anything about it.

Chapter 6: Saving Tomorrow For Another Day

I knew the moment I stepped on the campus of our local community college that I would never graduate. There was something inside of me that felt a deep opposition towards the entire idea. But the pressure of others' expectations for my life was enough to make me enroll.

I selected accounting as my major which proved to be an awful choice. I'm not even sure why I chose it; math had never been a strong suit of mine. Perhaps it was the idea of being able to say, "I'm Zak Maiden, *the accountant.*" I liked the sound of it. It felt like a strong choice, like something that would earn me respect.

But from the moment I stepped foot on campus, I hated every moment of it. Just the thought of sitting in a class where you might be called on at any moment brought a sense of dread and anxiety. All those eyes, all that pressure to know so many things. Despite the fact that I often drank and used drugs throughout high school, I had managed to get decent grades. I wasn't a bad student. But in college, I felt alone and exposed. For some people, the idea of the unfamiliar, the notion of exploring new friendships and experiences, is exhilarating, but it wasn't for me.

I lived in constant fear that the teacher would call on me or that a classmate would ask me a question. When I could focus, I could digest the academic knowledge. But I found it incredibly difficult to rein in my attention. I couldn't seem to connect with any of the my classes and I rapidly lost interest. It wasn't long before I realized that accounting was not for me and switched to another major. And then another. And then another. I hopped from major to major, hoping that whatever light seemed to switch on for everyone else, that thing that told them that they had "found their calling," would light up inside of me. But with each new switch, the light didn't come on and I felt more worthless and more defective than ever.

I took a job in construction while I continued to attend college, and that's when I had the bright idea of switching my major to Business Management, hoping that it would teach me more in an industry I already had experience with, and give me a solid path forward in my career.

Instead, it frustrated me.

I couldn't see any way that I would ever find use for what I was being taught in the classroom. I had worked a job since I was fifteen and most of the methods and information I was being taught didn't seem like they would stand a chance in the real world. I managed to make decent grades when I actually read the material and put in a little effort, but nothing I learned stuck with me. So, I started skipping classes, partying harder on weekends, and half-assing the homework assignments.

Deep down, I don't think I actually wanted to succeed. All around me were people who seemed perfectly happy to graduate high school, go to college for a few years, get a job, get married, and then work 8-5 for the rest of their lives. And the idea of living the rest of my life that way made me want to scream. But there is no easy alternative in our culture. You have the people who go to college and the people who don't. One group we deem successful, competent, and worthy of respect. The other we see as the misfits and outliers. The ones who just couldn't quite "make it."

My impulses told me to jump into the real world and build a life for myself in my own way. Earn it through sweat, grit, and hard work. I desperately wanted to be free from the constant social anxieties that school brought out in me. But the fear of what other people would say, what they would think, kept me going back.

In between classes, I'd walk with my headphones in and face pointed toward the ground, avoiding eye contact at all times. I'd go into the café and dart to the nearest empty table so that I could sit by myself. I looked at all the smiling faces and listened to the sound of their laughter and chatter. It looked so easy, so effortless - their display of making friends, flirting, and getting along with others. I didn't possess those skills unless I was drunk.

I needed Z-Man.

So one day at class, I grabbed a water bottle from my backpack and took a gulp. The strong flavor of the clear liquid sent a shock of surprise through me. It was vodka, not water - left over some night of partying that I had long forgotten. I mentally high-fived myself. I took another swig.

A girl next to me shot me a look of disgust.

"Umm, is that, like, vodka?" She looked incredulous, and the condescension in her voice was unmistakable.

With even just a few sips, I could feel The Real Zak slipping away and Z-Man taking control of me as my body began to buzz. I looked back at her, feeling frustrated and annoyed. The idea that a human being could so quickly judge and discount another was maddening. Had she walked in my shoes, faced my fears, or felt the choking stronghold of anxiety like I had?

"Does it smell like vodka?" I asked.

She stared at me blankly.

"Then it probably is vodka. Mind your own fucking business, bitch."

She smacked her lips together and ignored me. I took another drink. And then another.

My weeks became a blur of work, attending classes when I forced myself to, and then partying on the weekends with friends at neighboring universities where there were always generous amounts of alcohol and a variety of drugs to choose from. While I looked forward to the parties, I still felt anxiety in the hours leading up to them. The sober version of myself wasn't cut out for the party life - I was shy, timid, and afraid. That is, until I'd had enough to drink. And I always did. The Real Zak entered the party but Z-Man was the one who always walked out. Or *stumbled* out if we're being honest.

I knew that I would transform and become confident and brave. I knew I would become the life of the party. I knew I'd forget all about school, work, and fears for my future. It was simply a matter of administering the proper doses and blends of substances. It was the space in between that I hated so much. I dreaded walking into the party as the sober, scared, intimidated, awkward me, waiting to become something that was so much more. My social anxieties would clench even tighter than usual, choking me with an iron grip that only Z-Man was strong enough to break free from. And so I'd make a beeline for the alcohol and pound back drinks until the world began to drift away.

While it always started with alcohol, it never ended there. Alcohol was the gateway that swung open a wide path for drugs to follow. It was hard for me to understand how some people could drink without getting an immediate craving for cocaine or other substances. It was hard for me to fathom how people could dip their toe into the pool and not dive in. My goal was to transform from The Real Zak and into Z-Man. I accepted any pill or substance offered, hoping it would free me. Sometimes, I even brought Adderall or other things with me to make the process go quicker.

More often than not, I'd go too hard, too fast. In my panic, I would go from sober to incoherent in a matter of hours, completely bypassing the happily buzzed or even pleasantly drunk stage, the parts where friends or memories are made. I was always on the offense, trying to beat my anxiety to the punch, trying to strike first by drinking and partying before reality caught up with me and smacked me in the face, before it reminded me how lost and out of my depth I felt in my normal daily life.

I usually stayed out until 5:00 or 6:00 a.m. the following morning on the nights I partied. I'd sleep off my daze and pounding headache if it was a Sunday. I'd skip class if it was a Monday. On one particular day, I walked into my house in the early morning light, my body still floating in the haze of alcohol and substances. I knew I had classes in a matter of hours, but I didn't care. I planned to skip them and sleep the day away. But my mom was home. And awake. I knew I couldn't sneak past her or make up an excuse for skipping classes. So I got back in my car and drove to school. I felt happy and carefree on the drive. *This is the way to go to school,* I thought. I felt like I could take on the world. Z-Man was in the driver's seat and it felt good.

But by the time I made the thirty minute commute and had parked my car, I could feel Z-Man slipping away. My confidence and carefree attitude began to fade and my head began to pound. My stomach turned. I got out of the car and started walking toward the classroom. *If I keep walking it won't be so bad,* I thought. *Maybe Z-Man won't completely leave. Maybe I'll actually enjoy class for once.*

But each step I took slammed an icepick into my temples. Saliva pooled in my mouth and my stomach roiled. I crossed a small bridge, trying to stabilize myself but I couldn't. I bent over and heaved. Vomit spewed across the middle of the walkway. It burned my throat and pushed through my nose. The sound of my retching could be heard across the campus and several people looked my way in disgust. But I couldn't stop it. My ribs ached as I heaved again and again until I had nothing left.

I wiped my mouth with the back of my hand and looked around, my body crying out for somewhere to lie down. I spied a park bench not far away, the one that I often sat on between classes. That would do. I stumbled to it and I laid down, curling my body inward. Within minutes, I was asleep.

This was how it was when Z-Man left.

He showed up with the promise of making me powerful. I felt blissfully dazed and detached and my mind finally felt free. My thoughts didn't race, my heart didn't pound when someone approached me in conversation, and I didn't feel worried about the future. I laughed. I danced. I had interesting conversations with people.

But he always left me curled up in a fetal position. Sick. Alone. And, once again, anxious and afraid.

A year after graduating high school, I accepted an invitation to go to Ocean City again for Seniors Week, the same party I'd attended the year before, this time for all of the friends who were a grade behind me in school. We kicked off our first night away by making an extra-large batch of Jungle Juice - a mixture of lemonade, fruit punch, and, as you can imagine, shitloads of alcohol. We mixed it in a large white cooler and drank with abandon. Soon, the room was humming with music and loud, happy kids. The decibel grew as our inhibitions stripped away. It became so loud that several of us began to worry that we would be reported to the authorities. Most of us were not yet twenty-one, which posed a big problem.

My buddy hatched a plan to fake a cop raid. But then someone cranked up the music and *"The Lion Sleeps Tonight"* by The Tokens came on. I couldn't tell you exactly why that song triggered me, but within a few minutes I was butt-ass naked and dancing in the middle of the room with everything in me. My shocking display drove out half the crowd. No fake cop raid needed.

I didn't know it then, but that wouldn't be the last time I'd do that. Stripping down became something of a Z-Man trademark. Looking back, the irony is thick. The shyest, most insecure guy at the party is the one drinking the most, the one stripping naked. If I was the first one to put myself on full display, to show everything, there was nothing left for anyone else to expose. It was strategic. It was an odd way to grasp control.

After a while, I put my clothes back on and then poured Jäger into the pot of remaining Jungle Juice, transforming it into what we liked to call, *Death Juice*. At first, my friends thought I was pissing in the pot as the Jäger began to trickle in. They quickly realized it was just Z-Man taking things to the next level like he always did.

The next day, my friends and I continued to drink that Death Juice and lay on the beach - so drunk that we ceased to even have the ability to have a coherent conversation. Other friends of ours gave us a full report of our actions that day, all the things we didn't even remember doing - like having a full five-minute conversation saying nothing but made up gibberish words, trying to make out with a mannequin, and picking a fake fight with a five-year-old kid on the beach.

I relished the tales, adding more items to Z-Man's list of accomplishments.

Everyone liked Z-Man.

Everyone wanted him around.

All I had to do was make sure he made an emergence at the party.

At least that's what I believed.

But Z-Man also had a dark side when he was around for extended periods of time. When I drank, snorted, and swallowed enough, I moved beyond *Z-Man The Party Man* to *Z-Man The Incoherent*. The darkness would begin to show. I would turn mean and my tongue would lash out with razor-sharp words. I would insult people. I was verbally abusive to the girls who I attempted relationships with. As I did these things, I could feel The Real Zak inside, trying to resist these behaviors. There were times that I could feel my mouth opening and I knew exactly what Z-Man was about to say. Inside I would scream, *"Don't do it! Don't say it! Keep your damn mouth shut, Zak."*

But Z-Man would always win.

And I would cringe at the sound of my own voice cutting through someone like a knife.

But Z-Man's dark side wasn't just angry and hateful. Other times, as the night turned into morning, all that party happiness would subside and a deep sadness would envelop me, a depression so deep it left me lost and rudderless. The blackness of those times, the hopelessness that pressed into me, was unbearable. Sometimes Z-Man would cry or stare off into space. Other times, he handled the darkness by more visceral means. One night, after hours of drinking and doing several lines of cocaine, the darkness began to set in. For a while, I sat, staring off into nothingness. Then Z-Man whispered.

"Get a knife."

At first, I didn't stand up. But the voice, though inaudible, grew stronger.

"Get a knife."

Something weak and feeble inside of me tried to resist the idea, but The Real Zak was buried so far beneath the suffocating layers of alcohol and drugs that he didn't stand a chance against Z-Man.

I grabbed a knife.

"Cut.

It's the only way.

You have to feel something."

I pricked the tender flesh of my skin with the sharp blade. As promised, it sent a wave of feeling through me. The bodily sensation mirrored the feelings inside my mind and heart. As the initial pain subsided, I felt a small sense of relief, as if the darkness and pain had found an escape.

I suspended the knife over my skin again, gathering the courage to go deeper.

I plunged it in again.

At the sight of red blood, I knew I'd gone deep enough. I winced briefly at the pain, waiting for the release that followed as the red poured out. When it came, I put the knife away and covered the small wounds. That was the way Z-Man handled depression. The same way he handled everything. He was ruthless, harsh, and ferocious. He only knew excess and extremes.

Sometimes, in the space between the unpredictable and erratic behaviors of Z-Man and the anxious state of my sober existence, The Real Zak would manage to emerge. Deep down, I was a kind person. I felt a deep sense of empathy for others. And in between the antics of Z-Man, sometimes it showed. One night at a party, I saw a young looking girl sitting in a corner, looking pale. It was obvious that she wasn't accustomed to the party scene. I could tell just by looking at her that she was out of her depth. Suddenly, her face pulled tight and the color drained from it. She bent over and vomited on the floor.

Everyone watched her as she threw up and began to roar. They doubled over, laughing, pointing, and making fun of her. She was a spectacle, the center of attention, the low-hanging fruit for drunken mockers to pick. I saw tears welling up in her eyes as she looked around. I knew that look. She felt worthless. She felt like an outsider. She was the center of attention and she was hating it. I had felt that way more times than I could count. And I couldn't bear to watch it.

I walked across the room to where she sat and bent over the contents of her stomach that lay on the ground.

"Don't worry," I whispered. "I'll take the heat off of you."

I tried to think of something crazy, something unexpected that I could do that would turn all those eyes my way instead of hers. In the pool of her vomit was a lump that looked like the remains of a french fry. I grabbed it and tossed it in my mouth and swallowed. Everyone looked stunned and then erupted in horrified laughter. That would be the story the next day. Because the guy who eats a french fry out of puke is far more memorable than the young girl who can't hold her liquor at a party.

The majority of the time, The Real Zak and Z-Man were polar opposites in every way. They each had their roles, they knew when it was time for The Real Zak to get work done and when it was time for Z-Man to take over for the party scene. Sure, they collided at times, but they were never at war. Not yet. Because The Real Zak still wanted relief, wanted someone to take control, wanted to feel numb and free.

That was worth the pain of hangovers. Worth having to witness the impulsive choices that Z-Man made with my body - the self-mutilation, the stripping down naked and humiliating myself, the verbal assaults enacted upon others. I didn't like it. Sometimes, I wanted it to stop, but that would mean saying goodbye to Z-Man. What would my alternative be?

I wasn't willing to operate in my social world as the shy, timid kid I used to be. Not after I knew what it was like to feel larger than life and invincible. I knew I was smart and had dreams and drive for my life, but I couldn't fit myself into the mold that had been handed to me. I didn't have a sure career path, and I didn't know exactly who I wanted to be or what I wanted to do with my life. But I had Z-Man. And he was the life of the party. He was memorable. He was the guy who bought everyone the next round of shots and cocaine to share. He was the one who could handle more alcohol and liquor than most people thought possible. It was a talent, a gift. It had become my reputation, what I was known and respected for.

In the real world, I felt insecure and afraid. I felt worthless and unsure. I was insignificant. I was nothing. But in the world of parties and drugs, I was confident and brave. It felt like something when I had nothing. A party scene can become a little universe all to itself, complete with celebrities and legends, those who are willing to push their bodies to the extreme. They are the ones who earn respect. Somehow, because they drink more, snort more, and do more, they are the ones who hold the power. When I unleashed Z-Man, that's who I became, and it felt good.

And it felt good. My whole life I had felt powerless. I was the kid who couldn't hold onto his lunch money when the bullies asked for it. I was the guy who had his virginity taken by a girl he barely knew on a couch. I was the guy who couldn't even attend college classes without being riddled with anxiety. And I wasn't ready to face those demons on my own. I wasn't ready to cope without the help and influence of the substances that had the power to alter my entire being in a matter of moments.

So I let Z-Man take over without a fight. I let him use and abuse my body; I granted his every request to push my body to its limits. Sometimes, it felt like it was the one thing I really had going for me. I was young and my body was resilient, even in the face of the violent tug-of-war that I put it through between my sober world and my use of drugs and alcohol. But as time passed, my sinus cavities began to decay from the constant cocaine use. I felt muddle-headed and hazy more often than not. It was still a price I was willing to pay.

The years that follow high school are meant to be some of the most pivotal ones in any person's life. It's where you begin to find who you are, step into your identity, and become yourself. It's a time when you should be on a path of discovery and curiosity, a time to set your compass and plot a path for life. It's a time when you're supposed to get to know people and form deep relationships with others. Even more importantly, you're supposed to get to know yourself and form a deep relationship with who *you* are.

But it's hard to form a relationship with two different people. It's hard to know what you want to do and where you want to go when two forces pull in opposite directions within you. It's hard to think clearly when your mind is constantly altered and numbed.

From the outside, I appeared to be in a holding pattern, not really going anywhere in life.

The Real Zak just wanted one more night free from anxiety, one more night of feeling accepted, one more night of blissful nothingness before having to face real life and real challenges on his own. He thought he was just putting off decisions until tomorrow. He thought he was just having fun. He thought he was still in control.

Little did I know just how pivotal those years were. Little did I know that I wasn't just pushing away tomorrow, but actually choosing a path for my future and barreling down a course that would alter my life.

I still thought it was just fun and games.

I thought I could stop any time I wanted to.

But Z-Man was just getting started.

Chapter 7: Twenty-One

Though a handful of experiences stand out to me from teenage years and early twenties, most memories are hazy at best, swirling in a dark space of snapshots and vague impressions. They are out of order and hard to be certain of as I look back. And I don't believe that is by accident. I didn't want to live in real time. I craved the haze, so I created it.

But there is one day that I remember with perfect clarity. My 21st birthday. The day you turn twenty-one in Millersburg is the day that the rest of your life begins. By the time you reach that momentous milestone, you feel like you've waited a lifetime. No one actually expected you *not* to drink before your twenty-first, but you aren't fully welcomed into the social scene until then.

In Millersburg, there are those who go to church, those who go to bars, and a few who do both. But you'd be hard pressed to find a thriving social community elsewhere. On your twenty-first birthday, you are finally ushered into that community, the people who will be your tribe for the rest of your life if you stay in Millersburg.

In high school, kids were always talking about how they wanted to get out of Millersburg and go somewhere else. A few did actually move away and start a new life in another place. Most attended college for a few years then dropped out, moved back to Millersburg, and joined the workforce. It might surprise you how many people stay in Millersburg for life. There is a rhythm to that small town, a beating drum that everyone seems to live their lives by. Work hard, play hard. Work hard, play hard. Work hard, play hard. You live for the weekend, for the next party, for the first sip of alcohol sliding down your throat that tells you that you've made it through another week.

In many ways, the men you see at forty- or fifty-years-old sitting at the bar resemble the young men who walked through the doors at twenty-one - only now with wives and jobs they don't like all that much and wrinkles tallying the number of weekends they've made it to. They still talk to the same friends, tell the same jokes, curse the same job. Your 21st birthday is a rite of passage, a coming-of-age celebration, an initiation into this community. The day your life truly begins.

In line with the Millersburg custom, we planned to go out and celebrate at the stroke of midnight, so that alcohol would grace my lips the moment the day turned over. My birthday happened to fall on a Friday night that year, making it the perfect time for the event. No one would have to wake up and go to work the next day, so there would be plenty of time to sleep off a hangover. On top of that, it was Saint Patty's Day, which meant that the whole town would be out partying.

I was nervous all day as I anticipated my night of initiation. I had been blackout drunk more times than I could count, I had popped every pill and snorted cocaine. I wasn't nervous about getting wasted because I had done it a hundred times already. I was nervous because I knew that I wouldn't just be drinking with friends from college and high school. I'd be drinking with all the adults I had watched and respected all my life. This is the time to show what I was made of, to show that I was a man who could hold his own. I didn't want to be called "*a square*" or "*a pussy*" like others I had seen who either couldn't hold their liquor or didn't drink.

As the hours passed and midnight drew closer, my heart pounded.

"*Relax, Zak,*" I told myself. "*This is your specialty. If you drink hard and you drink fast, you'll be okay. Z-Man will show up. You'll be confident. You'll be the life of the party. Everybody loves Z-Man.*"

When the hands of the clock hit the stroke of midnight, my dad, mom, and brother whooped for joy. I had made it. I was on the other side now. They took me to The Moose, one of Millersburg's private clubs. We didn't enter through the front door which faced the street, but went through the back door, using my dad's exclusive member's key to get inside. As the door swung open, a faint din of voices and music washed over me, coming from upstairs where the party raged on.

I climbed the two flights of stairs that led to the club. The music and sound of laughter grew louder as I followed my parents onto the packed club floor. To my right, a large horseshoe bar curved around the well-stocked collection of liquors and then extended to a large back room where there were tables, chairs, and room for band equipment. I looked anxiously at all those bottles behind the bar, knowing the freeing power they contained. I was ready for Z-Man to take over, ready for my nerves to calm.

I scanned the faces around me. I knew almost everyone in the crowded room. Friends my own age and those a few years older, local business owners, friends of my parents. They were all there. Every age, every stage in life, all together under one roof. And it was my day to be a part. I felt unsure of myself and overwhelmed by it all. Within minutes, a shot glass was in my hand and I downed it gratefully. Then another and another as people stepped up to buy me a drink to commemorate the day Zak Maiden officially turned twenty-one and became one of the tribe.

It's about damn time, I thought.

I had always hung out with kids older than me - from the days with the eighth graders at the swimming pool until that very moment. Friends of mine would often use the weekends to enjoy what we called "2:30 blackout." We'd start drinking at 2:30 in the afternoon and get shitfaced by 6:00 p.m. But again, my friends were always older than I was and would go out to the club at night and I'd wait back at their houses. They'd always promise to be back in an hour and I would always wait for them, playing video games and drinking alone to pass the time, longing to be a part, wishing I were older. The group would return at 2:30-3:00 a.m. when the clubs shut down, and we'd drink together for the last few hours of the night. My age didn't hold me back from drinking, but it held me back from embracing the entire lifestyle.

So, as I looked at all those faces milling about on the club floor, the same ones that I spent so many nights waiting for, my anxieties faded away. They raised their glasses to me as the warmth of the liquor coursed through my body. I felt happy and accepted. This is the culmination of adult life in Millersburg.

And I had finally made it.

Round after round of birthday shots were sent my way. I was drunk within an hour and then wasted a few rounds after that. We left The Moose and made our way to The Legion. As soon as I walked in, I felt at home. Those walls represented so much of my childhood. It was a place that had been a constant in my life since the time I was young. I knew the bartenders, I knew the framed pictures on the wall. I knew the smell of crispy fried food wafting out of the kitchen, mixing with the distinct scent of cigarette smoke that hung in the air so thickly that even an hour or two within those walls would mark every article of clothing with its signature smell. I walked in proud and confident. I was 21 and this bar belonged to me now as much as any man in this town.

I spotted another group of friends who I knew at the bar and stumbled over to them, because that's how it is when you go out in a small town. Familiar faces everywhere, always someone to keep the party going, to do a shot with, to sit and drink with.

"Z-man! Come over and let me buy you a shot!" one of my friends shouted from the bar.

I didn't turn him down.

"What you need is a Four Horseman," he grinned.

"A what?" I asked.

"You'll see. Trust me."

The Four Horsemen of the Apocalypse is a combination of Jim Beam bourbon, Jack Daniels whiskey, Johnnie Walker scotch, Jose Cuervo gold tequila, and Jägermeister. Even if you are dead-ass sober, it would loosen you up. I was already drunk, and it's hard to tell the difference between drunk and *really drunk*.

"Let's do another," I said with the burn of the first shot still in the back of my throat.

And so we did another.

And another.

I drank over 30 shots that night and felt damn proud. Z-Man was no square and no pussy. He had just shown the world that he could hold his own. By the end of the night, I couldn't stand or walk straight. I fell over and a few of my friends carried me out and drove me home. There wasn't any other respectable way to return home in Millersburg on your twenty-first birthday except piss drunk.

The next thing I remember is my eyes fluttering open. I was lying in bed. By my side was a massive stockpot, reserved for making clam chowders or chili to feed a crowd. I groaned and lurched for it as vomit spewed from my mouth, the rancid flavor of Jägermeister pouring through my nose. As the clear liquid sprayed into the stockpot, my nostrils and throat burned. I vowed never to drink Jägermeister again.

A ding on my phone caught my attention and I glanced down to see a text from a friend of mine.

"Z-Man, we need a ride," it said. "Come and get us."

I managed to stand up. My balance was off but I managed to walk into the kitchen where my parents were. We chatted about the night before and then I stood.

"I have to go and pick up a few of my friends," I said. "I'll be back in a little while."

"Are you still drunk?" my mom asked.

"Nah, I'm okay," I said as I strode out the door.

Once inside the car, I congratulated myself on my abilities to hold my liquor and bounce back so quickly from such a heavy night of drinking. But as my car picked up speed driving down the hill, away from my parent's house, I felt a wave of dizziness. I was still drunk. Really drunk.

Looking back, I'm not sure why, after my twenty-first birthday celebration, it was me who picked up my friends when they were far older and more experienced. But, at the time, I'd do anything to be liked and accepted. I was the guy who'd buy the rounds of drinks, who'd pay for drugs. If you needed a ride, I'd give it to you.

Inside, I was still the kid giving away my cash at the swimming pool because I thought it made up for what I lacked. I felt like I lacked a lot. Z-Man was the guy who downed more shots, bought more rounds, took more dares, snorted more coke, and answered more drunk texts.

But The Real Zak? He was still anxious, unsure of himself and his place in life.

After I picked up my friends, we found ourselves back at the bar. And if you assume that it was deserted in the middle of the morning, you'd be wrong. All kinds of local clicks and groups rotated throughout the weekend. There was the evening crowd, the late-night crowd, the mid-morning crowd, the afternoon crowd, and so on.

I strode up to the bar and ordered a drink.

"You kidding me, Zak?" the bartender said. "You're like sixteen."

"Nope. I'm not. I turned twenty-one last night," I said proudly.

She looked unconvinced and I pulled my driver's license out in victory. She shook her head in disbelief and began mixing my drink. I now had plans for the weekend.

And every weekend after that.

Now that I could drink openly at the local bars and clubs, I didn't have to travel out of town for parties as often. I quit my college classes altogether and took a job at the local golf course. I excelled.

Being the shy kid who was always trying to find a way into social circles made me a master at learning how to do people favors and buy my way into their good graces, and this job capitalized on just that. I anticipated the needs of the people around me, I figured out how to speak their language and, above all, I knew how to keep the drinks flowing. I knew the power of alcohol. It set everyone in a good mood and it drove up the bill and my tips.

My social anxiety diminished while I worked that job, even sober. I felt protected by the one-sided nature of it. I was there to make *them* happy, show *them* a good time, and keep *their* drink glasses filled. They didn't really see me at all. They saw a persona, a character I stepped into by day, and I liked it that way.

With no college classes, my life fell into the same rhythm of those around me. Work hard, play hard. Work hard, play hard. Work hard, play hard. I existed through the week and lived on the weekend. Monday through Friday felt like sleepwalking, waiting to wake up and then blackout on the weekend.

With every passing month, I found myself partying a little harder. I frequented the local club and drank heavily, pausing every so often to walk to my car for a line of blow. Drinking made me crave cocaine. It was lost on me how anyone could drink and *not* want to do drugs. If a little was good how could you not want more?

I often partied for days on end, not even returning home to sleep or change clothes. I'd head to the bars at 5:00 p.m. on Friday and party all night and into the next days. Z-Man wasn't just emerging for a night here or there anymore. Now when he came, he stayed for days on end. Even the morning light didn't drive him away. After a hard night of partying, I'd order another round at 9:00 a.m. and continue to drink throughout the day. When night came again, I'd drink more, drink harder and bring out the cocaine. On the outside, I probably looked like a puffy-faced, greasy-headed shit face who hadn't showered or slept on those weekends. But as the alcohol pulsed through my veins and the effects of cocaine spread through my body, I felt invincible. This was my time to shine. This was my finest hour. This is what I was good at.

I felt like a hero. In some ways, I was. In a town where people worship the high school football quarterback and the man who can hold the most liquor, I felt like I was finally good at something, finally *worth* something. But my body paid the price for these moments of glory. Z-Man existed within my skin and bones and used me like a disposable glove.

One morning, Bloody Mary mix spilled down my shirt while I was out partying. Z-Man had no regard for my dignity or sanitation. I let it dry, staining my shirt like vomit. I sat in the mess and picked up cigarette butts, one after another, from the ashtray on the table. *And ate them.* No logical reason besides the fact that Z-Man wanted to try it. He was impulsive, animalistic, almost inhuman.

Another night, a friend vomited on my shirt. I brushed off the excess and kept partying for hours without a second thought. Another night, I crushed Vicodin into my drink as I mingled with others in the crowd. Another time, I drank nineteen Irish Car Bombs in the course of a day along with a handful of other mixed drinks. An Irish Car Bomb is similar to a boilermaker, made by dropping a shot of Irish cream and whiskey into a glass of stout. You have to down it in less than twenty seconds or the cream with curdle from the whiskey. I'll leave it to you to imagine what nineteen of those will do mixed together in your stomach.

The lack of sleep, the alcohol, and the drugs drastically altered my behavior and personality, causing me to act impulsively and erratically. I felt like a puppet with someone else pulling the strings. Some nights, I'd pull off my clothes and pretend to hump the ground. Some nights, I'd grab a stranger's breasts. My emotions had a mind of their own, rising and falling without warning. I'd go from dancing to weeping to yelling to laughing in the course of one night. It all depended on how the mix of substances I put in my body that night combined. Most of the time, I didn't remember what I had said or done the night before. People always told me stories the next day, filled me in on what crazy thing I said or did. The Real Zak was so buried and so numbed that he wasn't even conscious through Z-Man's weekend reign anymore.

A close friend of mine told me years later that he remembered me as being a blend of two different people during that time. Sometimes kind and caring, sometimes mean and hateful. Sometimes the life of the party, sometimes depressed and full of sadness. He told me a story of a time when he was struggling with the devastating loss of a family member to cancer. He told me that I sat with him for hours, talking about life and death and those we loved, comforting him and staying with him while others didn't. But several hours later, after I left his house to go to the bar, he said that I called him, blubbering and weeping. He couldn't make out my words and drove to the bar to check on me. He said that he found me, drink in hand, crying hot tears of anger. He tried to console me and convince me to leave and go home to sleep. But I refused. When he kept insisting, I grew so angry and agitated that I looked at him and slapped him across the face.

That is what life was like with Z-Man at the helm. I went from being a comrade and comforter to slapping my best friend's face in just a matter of hours. To be honest, I don't remember slapping him. I don't even remember why I was angry and sad. I used to live for the times when Z-Man would emerge, for the high that his confidence and bravado provided, but now when Z-Man showed up, he came in like a force, and I blacked out. No control. No idea of what he would do with my body while I was incoherent.

I only hoped I'd wake up when Monday morning came.

Somehow, I always did. I'd roll out of bed with a throbbing head, ejecting sprays of straight alcohol from my mouth.

The following days were tortuous as my body tried to recuperate from all it had been through - the excessive alcohol, the variety of drugs, the deprivation of food, the lack of sleep. As I suffered through Monday and Tuesday, I'd promise myself that I wouldn't go so hard next time, that I wouldn't do this to my body again. But by the time Thursday rolled around, even the idea of enduring another hangover was a fair price to pay for a weekend of partying. What else would I do with so much free time? Who else would I see besides the ones who would be partying with me? And so I suffered. Suffered through days of feeling like shit and to feel better just long enough to talk myself into blacking out and feeling like shit all over again.

Every time he came and then left, my body wretched and my head pounded. I would wake up and go to work in a fog. The cost of getting Z-Man to show up was getting higher and higher. Someone had to pay for the drugs, the alcohol, and the rounds of shots for the group, so that his reputation wasn't lost. These were the pieces that The Real Zak had to pick up when Z-Man vanished. My body was young and still resilient, but as the first few years of my twenties passed, I felt the toll it was taking on my body. My angular jaw rounded as my face grew puffier and my eyes dulled.

But in those days, I was still having fun. I still thought I could stop at any time. I still thought that The Real Zak was ultimately in charge. I still thought I was the one giving over control for a few days on the weekend for a good time. Z-Man was a party trick, he was there to make people laugh, make me feel brave, and bring me friends.

But after a while, The Real Zak stopped dreaming dreams for his future. He stopped trying to build a life. He existed for the nightmarish trudge through the motions of life during the week, sleepwalking until the weekend. He was growing weaker and more feeble by the day.

All the while, Z-Man grew stronger and bolder, especially with the newfound freedom that came with being drinking age. He wasn't content staying in the corner of my life. He wanted more. Always more. Another drink, another line, another pill. He wanted control. He wanted more of my time, more of my money, more of my body.

He wanted everything.

I had always believed that Z-Man was setting me free. Little did I know that he was tying me in chains, pushing me into an oblivion so deep that I wasn't even a coherent observer for the majority of my own life.

I thought my twenty-first birthday was when my life would truly begin, the day I would finally be free.

But it was the day that I gave up my freedom. The day I became a hostage inside of my own body.

Nothing more than a bystander.

Waiting to witness the end.

Chapter 8: And the Party Music Became a Death March

By the time my twenty-second birthday arrived, my primary goal in life had become making it to Friday night. And by the time my twenty-third birthday arrived, my goal in life was making it to Thursday night. My entire existence was a never ending cycle, a hamster wheel that I could not seem to get off of. Work Monday through Friday to make enough money to fund the weekend's events, and party all weekend. My body was in a perpetual state of either being under the influence of alcohol and drugs or trying to recover from the damage they had done.

The Real Zak rarely emerged anymore. His stamina to fight the impulses and habits of Z-Man grew weaker by the day. Z-Man only grew stronger and his appetites were insatiable. Not easily satisfied, his hunger for pushing the limits grew with every passing week. Now, a night of hitting a little Molly and getting blackout drunk was child's play and weekend parties morphed into seventy-two hour benders.

It always started with alcohol. I'd pound one shot and then another, just to grease the wheels a little bit before heading to the bar. At 5:00 p.m. we'd drive to Moose or Legion where we'd order cocktails and another round of shots. The alcohol would course through my body, giving way to a more powerful craving.

Cocaine.

Suddenly I would need it.

Right now.

I'd exit the bar, trying to look inconspicuous. Most knew exactly where I was going. In the front seat of my car, I'd roll up a dollar bill, and do a line. My nasal passages would burn, but no sooner than the earthy flavor spread through my mouth, I'd feel it. Total euphoria, dauntless strength. The drugs would temporarily push away the fogginess that the alcohol had created, replacing it with crystal clarity and total confidence. Which meant that I could drink more. Another round of shots and then another. I'd check my watch, wondering how the night had given way to early morning so quickly. Time seemed to vanish - like going to sleep and waking up hours later.

The club would close, most people ready to call it a night. I'd do another line of blow in the parking lot. Senses alert again, I would drive to whoever's house was open for the continuation of the party. We'd gather around a table or in a living room, minds racing with cocaine, and the conversation would begin to flow. We'd speak quickly and loudly, feeling brilliant and inspired. We'd bear our souls, share our secrets, pontificate life and the world around us.

"Just solving the world's problems, one line at a time," we'd say.

In the wee hours of the morning, nothing else would seem to matter, nothing but *that* moment, *that* conversation. That's what cocaine and alcohol does. It speeds everything up and slows it down all at the same time. It makes you feel like you're floating up above the world, looking down with total clarity while being completely engrossed in the present moment - every sound, every scent, every taste, every thought heightened. In those moments, I didn't think about anything. No thought for tomorrow, nothing but where I could get my next drink and line of blow.

And although nights such as these were dark and filled with choices I wish I hadn't made, I'd be lying if I said that these weren't also some of the best nights of my life. I want to say that those days were filled with nothing but pain and emptiness. Horror and depression. But though these elements were woven throughout my memories, they did not encompass the entirety of those experiences.

I met brilliant people around those tables littered with lines of cocaine. Some of the most brilliant people I've ever come into contact with, even to this day. I made deep connections around those tables and formed friendships like I'd never had before. We would talk about life and love. We'd dream about what the world could become.

What most people don't understand is that when you do a line of cocaine with someone, when you brave the night together side-by-side, there's a bond created. A bond that runs deep. Though looking back I can see that much of these deep feelings were manufactured by substances, it didn't make those experiences any less real.

I felt like I belonged. I felt safe, I felt confident. Though my body remained planted in Millersburg, my mind transported me into new galaxies of thought, realms far outside anything my sober, conscious mind was capable of. If you think for a second that everyone who does drugs is stupid, then you're just plain wrong. Some of the most brilliant minds, wealthy businessmen, and innovative thinkers I have ever met gathered around those tables.

When morning came, we would make our way to one of the private clubs, ordering cigarettes and cranberry vodkas to welcome in the day, though we rarely knew what day it was anymore. As the morning wore on and the high of the cocaine began to subside, I'd smoke cigarettes, one pack after another. I'd send a torrent of texts to my dealer, asking for more cocaine, knowing he wasn't awake yet. Z-Man always needed more. More alcohol, more drugs, more cigarettes. I rarely slept on the weekend or even changed my clothes. My hygiene was non-existent. My clothes smelled of sweat, alcohol, and stale cigarette smoke. My body was nothing more than skin and flesh, a human puppet to fulfill Z-Man's appetites and desires.

Time would begin to blur. I'd emerge from the walls of the club, surprised at the sunlight blinding my eyes.

What day is it?

Saturday?

Sunday?

Had one night passed or two?

I was never sure. My only concern was sobering up enough to go to work on Monday. As Sunday evening approached, I'd grow more aware of the clock. I'd check it, estimating the hours of sleep I'd be able to get before it was time to work.

If I go now, I can get six hours.

But then I wouldn't go home.

I really only need two to three hours at the most, I can stay a bit longer.

And I'd order another drink.

Shit, look at the time. One hour of sleep? That's rough. I can manage.

Even then, Z-Man didn't want to relinquish control. Didn't want the fun to be over.

"Tell them that your best friend just died and take the day off," he'd whisper.

And more times than I'd like to admit, I did exactly that.

The end had to come. No matter how much Z-Man kicked and screamed, fought and negotiated, the end always came. The handoff from Z-Man back to The Real Zak.

And the aftermath was brutal. As I would begin to regain full consciousness, I'd find a stinking, violently ill shell of a man. I'd have lost fifteen pounds over the weekend from dangerous dehydration and lack of eating any real food. Vomit would spew from my mouth and through my nostrils. I'd wipe my mouth and stand up in a hurry, sitting down on the toilet seat in just enough time to catch the bile that poured from my bowels. I'd hold my sides, as if the violence of my body's purge could rip me apart. My head would pound and the room would spin. After several hours, I'd pick myself up from the toilet and order something to eat. I'd gorge and binge, my body suddenly aware of its deprivation. I'd feel a bit better at first and then terrible all over again. My mind, emotions, and hormones would plummet and depression would close in from every side as the substances left my system.

And The Real Zak, beaten down, starved, and abused would emerge - feeling every painful moment of coming back to sober reality.

"You can't do this anymore, Z-Man.

You have to stop.

I can't suffer like this.

Not again.

Not again."

That feeble voice would cry and plead as my body would shake in the aftermath of Z-Man's leaving. But I had become his slave, only there to supply the funds required to fulfill his needs.

As time wore on, the effects of my lifestyle became more and more physically evident. My face grew round and puffy, my skin pale and discolored. My eyes sunk in and my midsection bloated. I hated my body. Z-Man abused it, stripped it naked at parties and humiliated it. He deprived it of food, water, sleep, leaving it depleted and writhing in pain.

I developed a visceral hatred for mirrors. I hated seeing the state my body was in. I couldn't look myself in the eyes. I didn't want to see The Real Zak, peering from behind the puffy flesh of my swollen face, trapped in a prison created by my own choices. I removed all the mirrors around my house, ensuring that I wouldn't see my reflection by chance.

But one night at a party, I ended up in a seat directly positioned across from a mirror. It taunted me, calling me to take a look. And so I did. I looked and then I kept looking. I couldn't pull away. I sat for what felt like an eternity to my drunken and disturbed mind, pulled into the vortex of my own eyes. Anger and hatred coursed through my body the longer I stared and a war began inside of me. Z-Man was angry at the pathetic, shy, weak excuse of a man chained somewhere inside the prison of my muddled mind. The Real Zak was angry that he had lost control, giving over body, mind, and soul to an abuser.

Suddenly, the rage collided, combusting from the inside out. I stood and walked to the mirror and punched my fist into the glass with all of my might. It shattered, breaking into pieces. Blood poured down my hand, but I hardly noticed. I could no longer clearly see myself. And that was all that mattered.

Z-Man was the local hero and the life of the party.

Z-Man knows how to drink!

Z-Man can hold his own!

Z-Man is crazy!

That's what they would say. But deep down, I knew my alter-ego was manufactured and severely limited. No matter how hardened and tough I appeared, I wasn't truly confident. I hadn't really changed. Z-Man was only the King in Millersburg. The moment I would drive out of the valley where Millersburg was nestled, all the familiar feelings of paralyzing anxiety would arise, making me feel like that shy little boy by the pool getting his money stolen, like the nervous college student hoping not to get called on in class.

But people didn't know that. I had created a persona, a larger-than-life character who had to be maintained. When my friends would brag about the new girls they would meet and their sexual conquests with them, I would play along as if I had fared just as well. In reality, I still couldn't talk to girls unless Z-Man had thoroughly buried all remnants of the shy Zak Maiden. I was still too afraid and nervous to strike up meaningful conversations on my own. So, I drank until Z-Man took the reins and talked for me. But he was loud, obnoxious, and wildly inappropriate. Nothing like The Real Zak.

I managed to form a relationship with a girl during that time but it was tumultuous from the start. One minute, we'd be together, and the next, we'd break up. What she didn't realize was that she was in a relationship with two people. One was wild, hot, jealous, overbearing, and unpredictable. The other was loving, sensitive, insecure, and riddled with depression. This created a toxic and ever changing environment in our relationship. We broke up constantly. Every time we did, I felt deeply afraid. Afraid of rejection. Afraid of being left to weather this monotonous world alone. I'd turn to cocaine to make me feel strong again and I'd party harder.

I wanted to be free, I wanted to break from my prison. But what would I do? Where would I go? I was still more afraid of being painfully awake for every moment of my life than sleepwalking through my days.

Hadn't I tried to make it on my own? Tried to battle through social anxieties? Tried to find a place to belong? Thoughts of the future only served as an unsettling reminder that I hadn't graduated from college, I hadn't found the love of my life, I hadn't discovered anything besides drinking to live for. I felt inferior and undeserving of a future. And yet, somewhere inside, I still knew that I was meant for something so much bigger than my small-town world could ever offer.

Z-Man's rampages, though destructive, were the only respite I had from my racing mind and the feeling that I wasn't meant for the world I was born into. I wanted to feel delirious and muddled. I needed the fog. I wanted to lose track of time, to float over my little world, to feel out of control.

I was running.

Running from myself as fast and as hard as I possibly could.

Just live in the moment. That's what people often say and it sounds good and wise and true. But while being wide awake and present for your life is a beautiful thing, there's also a dark interpretation of this adage. A sinister version where you induce a hypnotic, apathetic state, so immersed in the moment that even the concept of having something in the future to live for begins to fade.

And that's a scary thing.

Because hope is the knowledge that the sun will rise again tomorrow and that you have a reason to rise with it. Thoughts of tomorrow are what keep us alive. And when you cease to care whether or not tomorrow comes, you lose hope altogether.

My drinking and substance use began with a desire to feel free and gain confidence. But as the years wore on, the party music became a death march and I danced along - killing my future while I laughed and ordered another drink, too medicated and too numb to even care.

Chapter 9: Overtaken

Shortly after my twenty-third birthday, I met a beautiful girl. It wasn't love at first sight. In fact, we hated each other at first. We worked together and I got on her nerves and she got on mine. But the more I was around her, the more I felt attracted to her. She was only twenty which meant that she couldn't legally drink yet and wasn't allowed into the local clubs. She hadn't met Z-Man in all his glory - full of alcohol and cocaine. She knew The Real Zak, the small bit of him that still surfaced throughout the workweek. At least at first.

Our connection was real and authentic. She was aware that I drank and drank a lot. This fact was hard to hide with my reputation and habit of regularly showing up to work hungover. She didn't know about my drug addiction. I made sure to hide that from her. She came from a good family and I was certain they wouldn't approve of my lifestyle. I liked her. I loved how she laughed. We had fun together and enjoyed each other.

Until Z-Man started showing up.

Z-Man still wanted his seventy-two hour benders. He wanted cocaine by night and six cigarettes in the morning. He wanted blackout and oblivion. Girl or no girl, he wasn't going to give that up. But that lifestyle does not bode well for a relationship, especially one with a girl who isn't old enough to participate in it.

And so, for the first time, Z-Man and The Real Zak wanted different things.

This wasn't the first internal tug-of-war, but it had never been like this. Z-Man and The Real Zak had an understanding. They knew their places. Z-Man showed up when it was time to party and make friends. The Real Zak got work done and called mom and dad. But now, for the first time, I was pulled and pushed between two very different sets of desires, two very different paths for my life. I tried to do it all - be the good, hard-working boyfriend when I was with her and the party animal when I wasn't.

But that didn't last long.

My drinking and partying quickly became a topic of conversation between me and my newfound romance. She wanted me to drink and party less and to spend more time with her. I wanted that, too, at least a part of me did. But my willpower had grown weak against Z-Man. I tried to make feeble attempts to cut back, to make changes. But it only took one drink to give Z-Man enough strength to overpower me. One beer, then two beers, then shots, then cocaine, then more shots, then more cocaine, then blackout, then cigarettes, then more alcohol. The pattern was inevitable. Once my wheels started turning, I was a car without brakes. And I could never keep from rolling all the way down the hill.

For the first time in my life, there was a girl who actually liked The Real Zak better than Z-Man. For those few precious days when I wasn't completely altered and wasted, we would talk and we would connect deeply. She saw a side of me that few people did. The Real Zak was shy but caring, loving, introspective, and thoughtful about the world. In my rare moments of authenticity, we had a good thing going. Sadly, I can only remember a small handful of our moments together. Over the three years we dated, I have only a few concrete memories that I can hold onto because I was rarely sober. For the majority of my time, I was nothing but a sedated passenger, deliriously watching my life speed by with Z-Man at the wheel. I tried to hide it; I thought I could make both Z-Man and The Real Zak happy. But Z-Man was too strong. He rarely left me lucid enough to create memories with the woman I loved.

She wanted Zak.

The Real Zak.

For the first time, I was enough. I didn't need Z-Man to get the girl. But like a dark shadow, I couldn't shake him.

The night before my twenty-fourth birthday, I partied hard. Z-Man was in rare form. My girlfriend couldn't join me for the celebration because she had school the next day at a university located more than an hour away. This was sad news to The Real Zak but the best news ever to Z-Man. Now, he'd have full reign of the day and night. So I went hard. Shots, cocaine, more shots. I stumbled home in the early morning hours and crashed against my pillow. I awoke a few hours later, still drunk. I drove to a friend's house, anxious to get another drink in my hand. Z-Man had a full day of birthday plans ahead - golfing, drinking, and partying with no girlfriend in sight to kill the fun. I swaggered into my friend's home wasted from the night before and took a seat at the kitchen table. That's when I spied a bowl of dog food.

"*Eat it,*" Z-Man whispered in my ear.

Powerless to stop his drunken impulses, I dropped to my hands and knees and grabbed a handful of it and shoved it into my mouth. Everyone at the table laughed. They always did. Z-Man was the funny guy, the unexpected guy, the guy who knew how to entertain. My friend drove the group to the golf course where my birthday celebration was scheduled to continue. I walked on the course, not thinking of balls or scores, but of all the ways I was about to get *really* fucked up. I had a whole weekend to myself and I wanted to be blacked out by the end of it.

And then I saw her.

My beautiful girlfriend had managed to take off class so that she could surprise me on my birthday. She smiled brightly and searched my face, eager to see the happiness she hoped to bring me on my big day. Maybe The Real Zak would have smiled. Maybe he would have wrapped his arms around her and thanked her. The Real Zak loved her, but he was already too far beneath the fog of substances. The man she loved was nowhere to be found. She was no longer standing in front of her boyfriend. She was standing in front of Z-Man, and Z-Man had no use for her. He didn't love her; he loved his bottles and powders and pills.

Z-Man didn't even try to hide it. My face dropped at the sight of her. I felt nothing but sadness, disappointment, and anger as I realized that I wouldn't get to party as planned with her there. Z-Man had no use for the sweet, young girl who was a constant interruption to his plans. And so I just stood there, scowling. Pain slowly registered in her clear eyes and overshadowed her expectant face. She was hurt. And who wouldn't be? How do you begin to process the idea that the person you love is disappointed to see you? When you realize that the man you came to surprise would rather drink and party than spend time with you?

Still, she didn't walk away. She didn't leave. She kept trying.

We went to dinner but Z-Man made it clear that he was not happy. I sighed and cussed, acting like a certifiable dick to everyone, especially her. I refused to eat and slumped in my chair - angry that there were no shots of alcohol or lines of cocaine in sight. Angry that I had to endure dinner and conversations with people instead of celebrating the way I wanted to.

"Zak, it's your birthday. Don't you want to order something?" she searched my face for some hint of the man she knew.

"Fuck you," Z-Man spat out, looking the other way.

She stood from the table and walked outside the restaurant. I could see the tears welling up in her eyes. For a brief moment, even through the fog of my wasted state, The Real Zak surfaced. The sight of her through the restaurant window crying and the knowledge that the pain in her eyes was inflicted by the abuse of my words pained me. For that split second, The Real Zak rose to the surface, with feelings of love and remorse.

"Don't do this to her," The Real Zak begged.

But then the voice disappeared, taking all feeling with it.

As soon as she returned to the table, another stream of "Fuck you!" and "Fuck this!" poured from my mouth and I listened to the sound of it, powerless to stop.

Days like that exemplified the war that was constantly raging within me during that time. One day there was The Real Zak - the caring, introverted guy who loved people deeply. The next there was Z-Man - the loud, obnoxious, life of the party, whose tongue cut like a knife without caring who bled.

That relationship was just as tumultuous as my previous ones had been. We broke up and got back together multiple times. She was one of the only people who saw who I really was on the inside. I think that's why she kept returning to me throughout those three years, despite how badly Z-Man treated her. She begged me to stop drinking. She told me that things would be better if I didn't drink. And she was right. The Real Zak didn't want to lose her. He wanted to fight for her. He wanted a life with her. He had to try.

I can do it.

I can stop drinking.

I'll lose everything if I don't.

No more Zak, no more.

So I promised her I wouldn't drink. And for a whole month, I kept my word. And she was right, things were better between us when I was sober. We had fun together and our fights didn't escalate, they subsided quickly. We were bonded and close. Perhaps The Real Zak was strong after all. Maybe it was easier than I had imagined to sit in the driver's seat again and gain control.

But then her twenty-first birthday came. Innocently, she ordered a drink to celebrate.

What's the matter with having one beer? What's one piddly ol' beer going to do to me?

It's not like I have a problem.

I'll be fine.

So I ordered a beer and drank it. Then another one and then a couple more. And then I stopped. But I did the same thing the next night and again a few days later. That's when I felt it, Z-Man gaining strength again. Do you remember that scene in *The Incredible Hulk*, when Bruce Banner's heart rate begins to increase and you can see his muscles beginning to bulge and you know that the hulk is about to take over? There's that brief moment when you see it in his eyes, you can see him lose control. When he goes from being a shy scientist, to a destructive monster.

That's what alcohol did to me.

The moment it buzzed through my body, I could feel Z-Man rising up and getting stronger. It didn't take long before I lost control. The moment he took over, I went from slowly sipping a beer to downing shots and snorting cocaine.

Because Z-Man knew no limits.

Eventually, Z-Man won the battle completely. I couldn't stay sober. After my short month of sobriety, I found myself almost perpetually under the influence of some substance, making the moments when The Real Zak could be touched few and far between. Eventually, I lost the girl I loved so much.

Our final breakup only magnified the gnawing emptiness inside of me. I wanted love and acceptance, I always had. But from a young age, I felt that I wasn't enough to get it on my own. I felt too shy or too anxious or too odd or too nervous. I thought that if I was the kid with a pocket full of cash, I'd be able make friends at the pool. If I was the guy who stripped naked and shamed myself before anyone else had the chance to and made people laugh, I would feel accepted. If I was the guy who bought everyone shots or footed the bill for a line of cocaine, I'd be liked.

The Real Zak was empty because he actually wanted a life - something lasting, something meaningful. He wanted something he could grab onto and remember, something concrete that lasted beyond the next weekend or the next fix. He wanted love and acceptance. But Z-Man had grown too strong. He had built a reputation. He was the guy who everyone invited out. I wasn't ready to let that go. I wasn't brave enough to face the reality of what life would be like all on my own. I was still too afraid that no one would like me, no one would love me, no one would want to be with me. Afraid that if I brought The Real Zak to the party, everyone might turn around and walk away.

It may sound unbelievable, but despite how constantly fucked up my mind and body were, I took a position working for my father and was surprisingly successful at my job. I was smart, hardworking, and I made money. A lot of it, in fact. Z-Man loved to show it off. I wanted all the trappings. The nice car, the designer clothes, the jewelry, the new phone - anything to shout my wealth and status.

So I chased after all of it and more. But it still wasn't enough. It felt like I was pouring concrete into a well, only as soon as it reached the top and started to solidify and set, it would crumble away, as if the bottom was giving out.

This crumbling from the inside out made me a cold and angry person. I still have flashbacks of things that came out of my mouth during those years. My words were daggers that I didn't even know I was carrying. Those memories, like flashes from a nightmare, will always haunt me. They will always be my greatest regrets. Because I know that there is someone out there with scars on their soul that bear my name.

At times, I wanted to break free, I wanted to be done with drinking and using, quit for good. But I feared what life would be like without the presence of substances in my life. Who would want to hang out with a guy who doesn't drink? Would I be able to make friends? Would I be alone?

I didn't know and I didn't have the guts to find out. So, I kept going, kept repeating the same cycle over and over again. But the abuse, the damage that Z-Man inflicted, was getting harder and harder to bear. At times it felt as if he was testing the limits of my humanity, seeing how far he could stretch me before I exploded, seeing how far he could dangle my life over the edge of eternity before I surrendered.

As more time passed, Z-Man's erratic behaviors and biting tongue began to drive away my friendships. It's ironic, isn't it? Ironic that I began the drugs and the drinking as a way to make friends, to be liked, and to feel accepted. But as the claws of addiction plunged into me and invaded every aspect of my life, these became the very things that caused me to lose friends, lose love, and stole the fun and life out of everything.

As old friendships faded into the background, I formed a new connection with a man who was a bartender at The Legion. Not only did he like cocaine as much as I did, he actually *sold* it. This turn of events proved to be very convenient to my lifestyle. They say that birds of a feather flock together and that is true when it comes to addicts. After a while, fellow addicts are the only ones who will tolerate other addicts. No one in their right mind can peacefully coexist with the lifestyle of an addict or put up with the unpredictability of an addict's impulses, behaviors, and ever-changing emotional state. That's why toxic people attract other toxic people. Together, the toxicity is encouraged and multiplied.

After a few months of regularly hanging out, my new friend found himself tight on cash. He asked me for a loan and I was happy to help. I had money to spare and he only needed $1,500. As he looked for a way to repay the debt quickly, he came to me with an idea. Why didn't he just pay me back in cocaine since he had a generous supply of it? It was a win-win situation. I said, "yes," immediately.

Now, for the time being, I had an unlimited supply and was all too happy to take advantage of that fact. Knowing that I had a supply just waiting for me made my cravings emerge with a vengeance. I couldn't wait for the weekend to roll around to partake. So I started visiting him at The Legion during the day. He would serve me a drink and I'd slip out the back door and do a line. This pattern became a steady habit. And as luck would have it, I met another friend who dealt drugs of all kinds-- the kind of friend who was up for anything, ready to go along with even the craziest of Z-Man's ideas.

With these new friendships and my unlimited access to a large supply, Z-Man could not be relegated to the weekends. He wanted control *every* day. Cocaine made the foggy feelings of being drunk fade away. It made me feel alert, alive, and pulsing with life. It kept me going, kept me feeling superhuman, as if I had transcended the need for sleep or food.

But believing that you are superhuman is a dangerous thing.

One weekend morning, I sat at the bar inside The Legion, drinking a morning cocktail to shake off the fog of a night spent partying and doing cocaine. Two friends of mine broke out into an argument. It began to escalate, their voices growing louder and louder. Suddenly, I had an idea.

"I'm going to end this right now!" I yelled.

I slid off the barstool and walked outside. I unzipped my pants and began to urinate all over the vehicle that belonged to the guy who I felt was on the wrong side of the argument. I sprayed the sides, the door handles, everything. That was Z-Man's justice system at its finest.

My work completed, I made my way to my car and slumped in the driver's seat, barely conscious but preparing to drive anyway.

My friend ran to the car. "You're not driving, Z-Man," he said, pushing me out of the driver's seat. I mumbled something incoherent but complied and slid into the passenger seat.

As we drove away, two more friends hopped into the backseat and another argument broke out. There was yelling and cursing, cries of delirious people who had long lost the ability to reason logically or control their emotions. As the argument wore on, I looked down at the console between the two seats of my car and spied a coffee cup, still filled with old coffee from days ago.

"I have an idea," Z-Man whispered.

I smirked and grabbed the cup then slung it over my shoulder, squarely into the face of my angry friend.

Against all odds, our little angry, fucked up, and strung out crew made it to the golf course. I spoke loudly and angrily on the golf course, garnering the attention of the other golfers who had come out for a relaxing Saturday morning game. My father's friend owned the golf course and didn't tolerate rowdy behavior.

"Zak, let me give you a ride. You need to go," he said as he approached me, mid-sentence into some loud, drunken diatribe about who-knows-what.

I stopped for a moment and stared at him. If I had been sober, I would have been embarrassed and humiliated. I would have apologized and retreated to my car in shame. But that wasn't Z-Man's style.

"I'll let you give me a ride when you SUCK MY DICK," I shouted, staring straight into his eyes. "So FUCK OFF."

He must have known that I was drowning in a sea of substances. He must have known that I was beyond reasoning. He'd known me since I was kid, he knew my family, he knew that the facade I wore and the words I spat in his face weren't my own.

Despite my words, I did leave, along with the others who were with me, and we all headed to my truck. Still heavily intoxicated, I took the driver's seat and sped off the moment everyone was inside, heading for a spot on a mountainside near Millersburg that we liked to visit from time to time.

"I want to shoot your gun, Z-Man," one of my friends called from the backseat.

It's not uncommon to own a gun in our rural community and enjoying a little target practice was something that people often did. But a gun in the hands of Z-Man was a dangerous thing. The effects of the cocaine I had done only hours before still coursed through my body. I felt larger than life. Invincible. Superhuman. My mind was on high alert and yet somehow dark, mushy, and numb at the same time.

"You mean this gun?" I called out.

I grabbed the pistol in the front seat and pointed it out the window. I pulled the trigger and fired. Once, and then again. And again. The force of the bullet snapped my wrist back just slightly but I kept driving, maneuvering the wheel of the car at 45 miles an hour on the narrow dirt road up the mountainside. Cheers of disbelief and laughter at my sudden behavior broke out from the back seat. We'd outdone ourselves yet again. We were drunk out of our minds, high on cocaine, speeding up a mountain while shooting a gun. The car bumped and bounced as we drove. We were flying high with the thrill of doing something crazy.

Once we arrived at our spot, I threw the truck in park. We piled out, falling all over each other and proceeded to fire our guns off the side of the mountain, cackling in our stupor. Eventually, we made it back down the mountainside and into town - ready for another round of drinks. I walked into The Legion, ready to be served, but was promptly kicked out as word of my public urination had spread. I wasn't fazed. We just drove to another bar.

Another round of drinks, another line.

Then I blacked out.

The next thing I remember, I was blinking my eyes, trying to emerge from sleep. My friends stood over me, laughing, asking me if I remembered the things I had done the night before. When I shook my head, they proceeded to fill me in. They said I wadded up a pile of dollar bills and tossed them in a pile on the floor, unzipped my pants, and pissed all over them.

Looking back, this story is deeply metaphoric. I lived in a black oblivion while my body continued to move under the control of another force. Z-Man's irreverence and his visceral apathy for anything beyond the thrill of the moment led me to stand and literally piss on the building blocks of my future.

These memories come like snapshots. They come in flashes. I have one of leaving a whole bag of cocaine at a bar, realizing it, and going back to get it with no thought for how my future could be in jeopardy if I were caught. I determined that I must have put it in my cigarette pack, which had been thrown away in the large dumpster behind the restaurant. My friend held my legs as I dove into the garbage like a rabid animal, craving my fix.

Another recollection finds me with my nostril against the floor, trying to snort the remains of a line of cocaine that had been dropped.

In another, I am in the passenger seat of my 2016 Silverado at the top of a hill, throwing back my bottle of Corona, guzzling it until it is empty. My friend floors the gas and we race down the street and smash bottles against road signs, laughing as they shatter. The sun shines bright overhead.

Z-Man is already in full force by noon that day. I spy another hill and suddenly an idea springs to my mind.

"Wouldn't it be fun to ramp this car?" Z-Man whispers. I inhale, feeling the superhuman rush.

My friend agrees to do it but starts to panic at the bottom of the mountain.

"Come on!" I shouted. "FLOOR IT!"

He does and the car picks up speed. As it does, my friend yells, "I don't think we should do this!"

I smashed his foot down on the gas. Over the hill we speed and the car took flight, just as I predicted it would. We went weightless and then crashed back down to Earth, flying off the seats. I laughed hysterically. Flirting the line between life and death was just a game to Z-Man. After all, he had no plans for the future, no meaningful relationships, nothing to leave behind. My body was a disposable suit, there to carry out his wishes, something that could be tossed aside at any moment.

Another snapshot, it's been 24 hours of partying, and I receive a call from my mom.

"Zak, something is wrong," she says and tells me about a family emergency.

"What do you want me to do?" I ask her. I can barely think or form words through the fog of drugs and alcohol.

She tells me that she thinks everything will be okay but I can hear the worry in her voice.

Something in me snaps and I call out to my friends, "Listen up guys! Tonight we are going hard. VIP table. Bottle service. All of it. Let's PARTY!"

I sit at the VIP table and bottle service comes. I don't even bother with a glass. I grab the bottle and down almost half of it, gulp after gulp. And then I black out again. Snapshot gone.

Next slide.

I wake up to tales from friends who witnessed everything I was too drunk to remember. They tell me that I fell down a flight of stairs and caught myself on the shirt of a girl at the bottom. She was upset and two of her male friends jumped in to fight me. The bouncer kicked me out. They tell me that I stumbled out the doors and instead of fighting the men, I fought the curb, falling and slamming my head.

I look down at my ripped shirt, scraped and bloodied knees, and torn clothing. Proof of the entire story. For a moment, my mind parts enough to feel deep shame and embarrassment. My ripped clothing and bruised knees are proof of the shape I am in. Proof of the self-inflicted abuse my body endures, the pain created by choices that I don't even remember. I don't know how to cope with these feelings. So I do the only thing I know how to do when things get rough. I hop in the car and drive to another bar and party for the rest of the day. I don't even bother to change clothes. Once alcohol courses through my body, Z-Man takes over the narration of the story. He brags about the incident and shows off the scraped body like a trophy. I drink and then drink some more.

Until everything goes black again.

And I don't remember.

It's a strange thing, when everything goes dark and you are overtaken by another being with its own set of desires. It's strange to be informed of your own actions after the fact because you can't even remember.

But maybe that's all that The Real Zak could hope for anymore. He'd lost love, friends, and purpose. Rarely was he released from that foggy mental prison and into the light. A light which only illuminated the grisly aftermath of Z-Man's choices, almost making the darkness seem preferable.

Darkness.

Silence.

After a while, that's all I wanted, that's all I craved.

Darkness that would never end, silence that could never be broken. I was too weak to regain control and too afraid to witness the destruction of my own life.

I just wanted to turn out the lights.

And hide.

Darkness... It started to feel like the only choice I had left.

Chapter 10: The Gun

On April 22, 2018, I stumbled into my house at 4:30 a.m. It was Sunday and the night was giving way to morning, though I was none the wiser. I had partied all week long. Z-Man had now laid claim to almost every moment of my life that wasn't spent working. I slowly crawled through the door and my body cried out with the effects of countless days spent under the strain of Z-Man's choices. My mind was murky - as it always was after an extended bender. The mixture of alcohol and drugs blended together like a poisonous cocktail, flowing into every fiber of my being.

I sat down, my shaky legs thankful for something to hold my swaying frame. My body was both achy and numb. My mouth was parched. My senses dulled.

I needed to be still for a moment.

Something was clawing up from the depths of my mind... A thought, a feeling? I wasn't sure. But I felt it. It pulled at the thick layers of darkness that hung over me, fighting to form into conscious thought. I'd heard it before. Like snatches of sound carried through the wind that never form into words. Like liquid that slips through fingers when grasped.

It was me, my truest self, The Real Zak still buried somewhere deep inside trying to speak, fighting to be heard. But the substances that flowed through my body dampened the sound like a muzzle, turning my words into the guttural utterances of a drunk man - incoherent, not worthy of being heard.

But then I felt it. I felt it more than I heard it. The questions, the anger.

When did I become a prisoner in my own body? When did I surrender to the will of the darkest part of me - the bully, the tyrant, the oppressor?

How could I ever have believed that freedom existed in the bottom of a glass and in tiny piles of white? How could I have missed the clicking sound of chains, binding me into a vicious cycle of addiction?

How could I have not realized that this alter-ego, this superhuman version of myself, would one day hold me hostage inside my own body - demanding me to sacrifice one more night, one more relationship, one more piece of myself until there was nothing left?

These questions did not surface in coherent form, but in feelings that coursed through me like blood. All I knew was that I could not live another day as a prisoner within my own body, abused and tortured, nothing but useless collateral along the way to the next thrill.

I had tried to stand up and fight him before. I tried to say no. But my will had grown weak and I felt powerless to fight the chains of my addictions.

These thoughts began pushing up through the surface of my consciousness - through the darkness, through the bars and walls that held my mind captive.

And then finally, I could hear it.

My own voice.

The Real Zak broke through all the fog and uttered three simple words.

I am done.

I thought that I needed Z-Man. I thought I needed him to speak for me, make friends for me, calm the storms of anxiety for me. But I suddenly realized that he needed me, too. His voracious appetite needed a willing body and willing mind that would bend to his desires and give into his lusts.

And that's when a sense of resolve settled over me. Suddenly, I knew with absolute certainty that I'd rather choose total silence and complete darkness than spend another day at the mercy of this oppressor. I'd rather disappear completely than witness the destruction of life from behind my foggy prison or listen one more time to my mouth lash out hateful words like razor blades, slicing those I loved.

Z-Man had taken everything from me and I had allowed him to. He had stolen the best years of my life, destroyed my relationships, wrecked my body, and sacrificed my future on the altar of his desires.

But I did have one choice.

One thing that would silence the bully forever.

I am done.

Stringing together those three words through the fog and into coherent thought took all the strength I had.

I rose to my feet and opened the drawer where I kept my gun. I grasped it, my fingers folding around it, feeling its weight in my palm.

This was my key, my chance to break from the prison of my own mind.

I couldn't back down now. I settled myself back into my chair and cocked the gun without pause. I didn't stare at the bullet in deep contemplation. I didn't breathe heavily or cry.

I just took a deep breath.

Pointed the smooth barrel into the flesh of my temple.

And I pulled the trigger.

I waited for darkness to follow, for the silent black to envelop me.

Instead, I only heard a click.

And another breath passed through my lungs.

I pulled the gun down in front of my face. Had I forgotten to put a bullet inside? I cocked the gun back to see. And a bullet popped out.

I should be dead right now.

I should be dead right now.

I drew in another deep breath and then another. I was alive. And I felt different.

The power had shifted. I had taken a stand against the bully. And a feeling washed over me that I hadn't felt in a long time.

I was at peace.

I placed the gun back in the drawer and walked up the stairs and slept like a rock.

The next few days were strange. I wasn't sure how to process what had taken place. I felt like I had the upper hand, like I might just be able to fight my way to freedom. The Real Zak had gained enough strength to fight, to fight for life. Out of habit, I had a few alcoholic drinks throughout the week, but didn't party hard. Something was different.

A battle was brewing inside.

Six days later, I woke up early. I blinked, pushing away the drowsiness. And then a moment of clarity struck me, almost as fast as the morning light hit my eyes.

I was in a position to take control. I had the key to unlock my own chains.

But I had to face my oppressor.

It was now or never.

It was time to face myself.

I got out of bed and walked to the nearest mirror I could find. I had broken or turned most of them to face a wall. I didn't want to look myself in the eyes. I didn't want to see the space where both The Real Zak and Z-Man existed.

But this time I stood squarely in front of my reflection.

And I looked.

I looked at my puffy, discolored face. I looked at my bloated body. And then I looked deep into my dull, bloodshot eyes as they stared back. I hardly recognized myself.

I was eye to eye with the bully now.

A moment passed and I drew in a breath.

And then I let it all out, all the things I wanted to yell and scream for months and years while I sat like a silent bystander to my own life.

"YOU FUCKING COKEHEAD, YOU FUCKING PIECE OF SHIT! LOOK AT YOU. LOOK AT WHAT YOU'VE DONE TO ME!

I HATE YOU.

I HATE YOU.

I FUCKING HATE YOU!

YOU HAVE A PROBLEM. A SERIOUS PROBLEM ZAK MAIDEN. AND YOU'VE GOT TO GET HELP!

YOU'VE GOT TO CHANGE.

BECAUSE RIGHT NOW YOU'RE A WORTHLESS PIECE OF SHIT."

I sat for hours in front of that mirror and I threw words like fists - fighting back against the bully who had held me down for so long. Tears streamed down my face and my throat grew raw from the torrent of screams. But I couldn't stop. The dam had broken and an ocean of pain and anger poured out. I lashed out, my words like brutal punches, delivering one blow after another without mercy.

I had always been the shy one, the quiet one, the anxious one. The kid handing over money to the bullies at school. The teenager who didn't know how to say no when his virginity was being stolen. The one riddled with social anxiety. I had always taken a seat, shut my mouth, rolled over and complied.

But not that day.

That day I stood up and faced the biggest bully of all.

I faced myself.

When I pulled that trigger, I wounded the bully even though my physical body remained untouched. But now I was taking my power back. My words pummeled him into the ground and for the first time in a long time, I was in control of my own life again.

I was battered and weak, like a dirty prisoner squinting into sunlight for the first time after years behind bars. I wasn't sure what to do next. But for the first time in a long time, I felt free.

I had to declare it.

I pulled out my computer and logged onto Facebook.

"I have a drinking problem," I wrote.

"A serious problem. I don't know exactly how to overcome this, but I'm going to put one foot in front of the other and I'm going to make a change."

I read it once and then pressed publish.

And that was the first day of my sobriety.

Chapter 11: The Hardest Goodbye

The weeks following that Facebook post and my decision to quit alcohol and drugs can only be described as... *weird*. It's not an eloquent word. It's not inspirational or powerful. But it's honest. Because in those first few weeks, I didn't feel wise or eloquent. I didn't see what I was doing as a good story or something inspirational.

I just felt *weird*.

For the first time in a long time, it was just me. The real, authentic, shy, small-town guy named Zak Maiden, trying to figure out what a life without drugs and alcohol was supposed to be like. Nothing there to alter, amplify, subdue or enhance me.

The week after my attempted suicide, I began tapering off of alcohol and didn't partake in any substances. This likely helped my body through what should have been a brutal withdrawal process. I had a few drinks here and there throughout the week and then made my final decision to get completely sober.

I was so accustomed to the pain of the abuses that my habits inflicted upon my body regularly that even the withdrawal was bearable. Still, my body screamed and cried out, pleading for relief. The Real Zak had gained the upper hand but that didn't mean that Z-Man was gone. He was still there. Only this time, it was his turn to plead and beg.

Just one drink.

Just one line.

C'mon, Zak.

I didn't fight these thoughts and urges with lengthy speeches about my future or tell myself that I was on the road to making some incredible transformation. I simply whispered back,

"If you don't do this, you will die."

I had no idea what my life would look like sober. I just knew that I wanted to live and live free. I was fighting for my life.

"If you don't do this, you will die."

One day at a time.

"If you don't do this, you will die."

One foot in front of the other.

"If you don't do this, you will die."

In those first two weeks, I found myself at a loss of what to do. All free time outside of work had been consumed with alcohol and drugs since I was a teenager. I had experienced my whole adult life through the lens of substances. And suddenly, there I was, a 26-year old man who quite literally *had no idea* what to do with himself.

What did people do to pass their nights?

How did people fill their weekends?

I had no idea.

The void was unnerving. The total awareness of each moment without the slippery, slidey, fogginess of drugs and alcohol made time feel slow, stretching out into endless space. A horizon without edges.

I didn't know where to start. I had no framework, no understanding of the process I was undergoing, no comprehension of the magnitude of what I was attempting to do on my own. I didn't have language or terms or twelve-step processes memorized. I was just a guy trying to stay alive.

I sat down at my computer and began to research everything I could find online about sobriety, alcoholism, and drug addiction. I googled everything I could think of. Stories about sobriety. Celebrities who overcame drug and alcohol addiction. Books on recovery. Movies about overcoming addiction. I ordered a handful of books and followed recovery pages and influencers on social media. I was hungry for guidance, a sign that I wasn't alone, a compass to show me the path ahead.

So, I used the time that alcohol and drugs had once occupied to read, research, work out, and watch movies.

For most of the week, I felt okay. Then the sun would begin to set on Friday evenings, and I would drive back to Millersburg from whatever job site I was working on during the week. That's when I would feel it. The urge to walk through the doors of The Legion and toss back a few drinks. To lower my nose to that little white pile of powder and rise with an inhale of super-human feeling.

My body knew, every ounce of skin and flesh knew, when it was Friday night. And I wanted to get *greasy*. Maybe that word sounds insane to you. But it's the best way to describe what it feels like to get in *the zone*, all blurry, hazy, murky, and mushy with alcohol and drugs. All easy, lubricated *yesses,* no inhibited *nos*. All apathy and no empathy. All confidence and no insecurity.

On those nights, my tiny hometown felt suffocating. When I didn't know what to do or where to go, I'd go to the gym. I'd sweat, mile after mile, on the bike - my mind devoid of any thought besides making it through another day. After an hour or two of biking, I'd lift weights until my muscles ached and my body pleaded for sleep. Only then would I drive home, shower, and crawl into my bed, exhausted.

During the time I wasn't at the gym, I filled my nights and weekends watching movies - especially those made in the 1980s and early 1990s. I searched for any movie I could get my hands on that centered around sobriety or drug recovery. The scenes in those movies moved me. They made me feel emotions that I couldn't seem to touch in real life.

There is a scene in the movie *28 Days* where Sandra Bullock plays a big-city newspaper columnist who is forced to enter a drug and alcohol rehab center after ruining her sister's wedding and crashing a stolen limousine. In it, a character named Cornell, played by Steve Buscemi, said the following lines:

"If that will make you happy, I will stop drinking. And then I would tell myself tonight I will not get wasted. And then something would happen. Or nothing would happen. And I'd get that feeling and you all know what that feeling is; when your skin is screaming and your hands are shaking and your stomach feels like it wants to jump through your throat. And you know that if anyone had a clue how wrong it felt to be sober, they wouldn't dream of asking you to stay that way. They would say, 'oh geez, I didn't know. It's okay for you. Do that mound of cocaine. Have a drink. Have 20 drinks. Whatever you need to do to feel like a normal human being, you do it.' And boy I did it. I drank and I snorted. I drank and snorted. I drank and snorted. And I did this day after day, day after day, night after night.

I didn't care about the consequences because I knew they couldn't be half as bad as not using. And then one night something happened. I woke up. I woke up on a sidewalk and I had no idea where I was. I couldn't have told you what city I was in. And my head was pounding and I looked down and my shirt is covered in blood. And as I'm lying there wondering what happens next, I heard a voice. And it said man, this is not a way to live. This is a way to die."

Those lines hit me with force. Never before had someone captured what I was feeling and put it into words so perfectly. Never had I heard anything that explained what the battle with alcohol and drugs *actually feels like* with such accuracy. I watched that movie time and time again with an ache in my soul, rewinding that scene multiple times. It embodied the battle that I had been fighting for years and it made me realize that I wasn't the only one with these struggles.

The more I read, watched, and researched, the more I understood what I was facing, and the less I felt alone. I wasn't a freak. I wasn't a mutation. I wasn't a fuck up. I wasn't broken. There were others out there who were facing all the same struggles that I was.

This realization pushed me to continue to post openly on social media about my struggles with addiction and recovery. Even if I could help just one person to feel understood and not alone, it would be worth it. The feedback was overwhelming. I was surprised by the number of responses that flooded my comment sections and inbox. People being supportive, people opening up about their own struggles, people feeling understood for the first time.

I will be the first to admit that social media has many negative aspects to it, but through those first few months of my sobriety, it was a lifeline. It gave me motivation, community, and connection with people at a time in my life when I was desperately lonely.

To be clear, it wasn't that my friends didn't call me or invite me out anymore.

They did, in the beginning at least.

"Zak, buddy, it's Friday! Time to get fucked up. Let's meet."

"What are you up to Zak? Me and the gang are meeting at The Legion, come join."

"Where have you been Zak? Come join us!"

My phone flooded with messages. Phone calls. The 3:00 a.m. texts. I said no to most invitations but actually accepted others. I felt like I needed to face my demons head on, not be afraid of hanging out with people or going into bars. Perhaps it wasn't the best idea given how feeble my new sober legs were, without enough time to make them sturdy enough to withstand temptation. But I didn't know. I didn't have a guidebook on sobriety. Facing my enemy straight on seemed like the best idea. So on the nights I didn't work out or watch movies, I'd go to the bars.

At first the bartenders would bring over my favorite drink and set it down in front of me like they always did. And I'd send it back.

"I'm not drinking anymore," I'd say. "I'm trying to quit."

Interestingly, it was the bartenders who respected that decision the most. They quickly learned that I was serious about staying sober and did their best to support that choice. A couple of times I ordered a drink out of sheer habit and had to send it back. The bartenders quickly took it from me and replaced it with water. Water was my saving grace. I drank it by the gallons on those nights, trying to quench the insatiable thirst inside of me. I felt nervous and shy, out of place and anxious. The very rooms that had once been so familiar, the same turf that I reigned over, were suddenly strange and foreign. I was an outsider.

A few friends were understanding and supportive of the major lifestyle change I was making. Others thought my newfound sobriety was simply a phase or some spontaneous attempt that would soon blow over, something that could be renegotiated with enough peer pressure. Others seemed to feel awkward around me and unsure of how to relate to the sober version of Zak.

I wasn't the same person that they used to party with.

Everyone knew Z-Man.

They knew the larger than life persona, the boisterous laughter and antics, the brazen and wild behaviors. And so the quiet, shy, brown-haired fellow sipping water and watching from the corner of the bar was a newcomer for everyone, even me.

Many friendships dissolved in the months that followed my choice to become sober. As weeks turned into months, it became clear to everyone that I was actually serious about what I was doing and that Z-Man wasn't going to come back.

And while many people applauded me, most didn't know what to do with The Real Zak. Alcohol is embedded in every facet of the social community in Millersburg, and as word spread that Z-Man was getting sober, many people seemed unsure how to act around me.

I think at times my sobriety was a reminder of something they had promised themselves they'd do a hundred times and never did. There was nothing in me that wanted to guilt or shame anyone and the only person I needed to confront was myself. I was barely holding on for dear life, barely making it another day. But the very act of remaining sober drove a wedge between me and many relationships. My existence became a confrontation even when I wasn't saying anything at all.

But of all the friends I lost, there were two who left a tremendous void in their absence. Two relationships I had treasured since I was barely a teenager. They had seen me through the best of times. They had celebrated my successes. They picked me up when I was disappointed or sad. They sat with me through the ugly aftermath of breakups. They were my wingmen when I flirted with girls. They comforted me through grief. They were my constant companions, my truest friends.

And their names were Alcohol and Drugs.

Almost every memorable moment in my life was shared with these two friends. They were a constant in my life. I never felt like I had to explain myself to them, they were *just there*. I didn't have to form my feelings into cohesive sentences for them because they never needed an explanation. I didn't have to bare my soul or confide my secrets because they already understood. I didn't have to strategize a way around my problems and challenges because they would make me forget. I didn't have to feel anxious because they would make me brave. I didn't have to feel pain because they always offered the perfect numbing agent to dull it.

And when I had to say goodbye to them, it felt as if someone had died. I lost the sense of confidence that I had grown accustomed to. I lost my primary means of coping. I lost my ability to say *fuck it* and force worry or sadness to go away.

Recovering addicts talk about withdrawals, they talk about the battle of sobriety, they talk about hating who they became as an addict, they talk about incredible transformations. Few talk about the sadness of losing everything that feels familiar. Few talk about having to let go of something you love. Few talk about having to grieve the loss of the person you were with those allies close by.

Sobriety comes with great loss.

After a few months, I found myself completely alone. No one seemed to want to talk with me or be with me. Many nights, I sat alone at home and cried. Tears rolled down my face for the phone that wasn't ringing, the text inbox that was empty, the parties that I was no longer invited to, the friends I had lost, and for the big, black void that was left where drugs and alcohol used to be. My greatest fear - the fear of rejection, the fear that The Real Zak wouldn't be enough for those around me - seemed to be confirmed.

But as time passed, I realized that many of the bonds I fought so hard to form and the people I tried so hard to be accepted by weren't worth the effort. I realized that my other two friends, drugs and alcohol, were fake, false, and toxic.

With an evil, slimy grin they whispered,

"We're your friends.

We're here for you.

We'll never leave you."

Before I broke free, that sick song had pulled me back into the dance of addiction time and time again. I was not only addicted to these substances, but also to the false sense of love and acceptance they provided.

At the time, I didn't have any sense of perspective to know what I was facing or feeling. The void seemed so great that I feared it would swallow me whole. It felt insurmountable, unsolvable, and unending. Because all I could see was emptiness. How do you go around, above, or through emptiness? How do you solve it or fix it or make it go away? The only thing I knew was that I had to live and I had to be free. And that meant staying sober and saying farewell to my two best friends.

And that was the hardest goodbye.

Looking back, all I can do is thank the young, clueless Zak who held tight when he had no idea what was going on. The one who kept taking steps even when he couldn't see where he was going. The one who ordered another glass of water while everyone else basked in the glow of alcohol. The one who shut his eyes and gritted his teeth when he felt as if a hundred bugs had invaded his flesh when the cravings would come. The one who said no to the screams and pleading cries of his body for just one more line, one more pill, one more drink. All I can do is thank him for feeling his way through that darkness.

When people talk about recovery, they want to tell you what's ahead, how amazing the view will be; they want to tell you how the light will pour in and how good it will feel to be on the other side. I could tell you all of those things. And I will.

But first, I need to tell you about the void, about the loss, about the loneliness. Because I want you to know that when you don't know what's ahead, when you can't see the view, when the light doesn't come, and when the journey feels anything but good, that you're not crazy, you're not broken, you're not weird. I want you to know that sobriety will feel like the loss of your best friend, it will feel empty and unnatural, it will feel like you're learning to walk again for the first time. I want to tell you this because I want you to be prepared. I want you to know that you're not alone. And I want you to know that it's going to be okay.

I can see the purpose in all of it now, I can see where the path was leading as I look back with the perspective that time offers. I wish I could have whispered in the ear of that young, scared version of myself that everything would be alright, that it was all part of the process, that it wouldn't always feel that lonely and empty.

I wish I could have told myself that the void, the emptiness was simply making room for what was coming next. Something that would be so much better than the deep rooted toxicity that once grew there.

So I'll tell you instead.

If all you can see is emptiness.

If all you feel is loss.

Don't run.

Fight through it.

Put one foot in front of the other.

It's going to be a long journey.

But, fuck, the view is gorgeous.

Chapter 12: All Better Now

Truth be told, I didn't know what the fuck I was doing when it came to getting sober and staying that way. The only thing I knew was that I had to stop drinking and doing drugs. That was it. That was the extent of my great emotional enlightenment. It was pure survival. I had no grid for the mental or emotional aspects of recovery. I had no thought of the demons that lurked beneath the surface of my mind, the ones that had led me down the destructive path I was attempting to come back from. So I focused first on what was tangible, what I could see. And my body was an easy target.

At 224 pounds, I was a five feet, eight inches blob. I had a puffy face and dull eyes. A pillowy midsection and weak arms. My body provided a problem and challenge I could touch. It was something I could alter and physically change. The gym became an outlet for me and I pushed harder as I narrowed my sights on this single focus. The droplets of sweat, panting breath, and aching muscles gave me a handle with which to touch and hold onto the transformation I was undergoing.

I didn't know how to heal my mind, but I could run on a treadmill for miles. I didn't know how to begin to unravel and release the weight of my issues, but I could sling iron until my muscles screamed. I watched weight fall from my body and lean muscle take its place, counting it like a metric by which to prove to myself that I was healing and changing. The dull haze slowly fell away from my eyes and a clear green took its place. It felt good to be able to see, touch, and feel how I was changing.

During that time, I came across an author and motivational speaker named David Goggins - an American ultramarathon runner, ultra-distance cyclist, and triathlete. He is a retired United States Navy SEAL and former United States Air Force Tactical Air Control Party member who served in the Iraq War. I read his book, *Can't Hurt Me*, a brutally honest memoir about his life and the nightmare of poverty, prejudice, and physical abuse that colored his days and haunted his nights as a child and then his rise beyond it through self-discipline, mental toughness, and hard work. I inhaled every line of the book, awed by the way he transformed himself from a depressed, overweight young man with no future into a United States Armed Forces icon and one of the world's top endurance athletes through pure mental stamina and grit.

I would listen to his voice through my headphones and walk for hours on the treadmill at the gym every day. His almost-vicious style kept me going, kept me walking another step. It kept me fighting, kept me engaged in the battle. Sometimes, my mind would go completely blank as if in a trance. No thought would cross my mind for hours, nothing but the command to put one foot in front of the other. Again and again and again. The only thing to break my daze would be the sudden shutoff of the treadmill, alerting me that I had reached the maximum time that it would allow for one exercise session. My fixed eyes would move to the buttons and I would tap them robotically until the motion under my feet began again.

For those first several months, I worked, I ate, I watched movies, I went to the gym. I clung to my routine like a safety net. Some days, everything felt okay and the prospect of facing a life without alcohol and drugs seemed doable. Other days were hard. I remember working outside one particular day with a group of installers for a bleacher renovation project that our business had taken on for a local school. I had purchased several expensive relays and set to work installing them. It should have been a simple task. But then the fuse on the first one blew. I felt my anxiety rising. I took a breath and grabbed another relay and set to work replacing the blown one. That fuse blew too.

Another wad of cash down the drain.

I felt my blood pressure rising. I grabbed a third relay and tried to calm myself as I worked through the tedious installation process yet again. I had done it countless times before and I could find no reason that the fuses should be blowing out. I surveyed the entire area and tried to find any explanation for why it was continuing to happen. I called over another installer and asked his opinion, double-checking to make sure I wasn't missing something. He couldn't find anything amiss either. I found the owner of the facility and explained what was going on and together we looked over everything, yet *again* just to be absolutely sure that I wasn't missing something. We didn't find anything.

So I tried again. And a third fuse blew.

Rage bubbled up in me. I had just wasted a significant amount of money on buying the relays and I still didn't have a clue how I was going to solve the problem and finish the job. I hopped into my truck and sat for a moment before turning the key. Suddenly, all I could think about was how much I wanted, how much I *needed,* to get fucked up. I needed the burn of alcohol down my throat to smooth the sharp edges of the day. I needed the snort that would usher me out of this nightmare and to the place where nothing seems to matter. My senses screamed for relief.

It's been a bad day, Zak. And you and I both know what would make this better.

That old, familiar voice whispered in my ear.

The same one that once promised to make me confident and fearless, likeable and free. The same one that had used my body like it was disposable and threw away years of my life into a pile of trash. I knew I couldn't give in. But the voice screamed louder.

Just one drink. Just one night. You don't have to feel this way. You can make it all go away. You deserve it.

I gripped my steering wheel, trying to silence the voice. I had fought so hard to take control and I had almost lost my life in the process.

And I wasn't going to hand it over.

I gripped that wheel until my knuckles went white, willing myself to drive to Planet Fitness instead of the bar. I pulled into the parking lot and jumped out of my truck without giving myself another minute to think and jogged to the treadmill. The motion started and I began to walk. I rebelled against temptation, against the impulses and voices in my head, with each step. As droplets of sweat poured from my temples, my mind cleared. My racing mind began to calm and the voices quieted down. I don't even know how long I jogged or how many steps I took. The next time I looked up, it was dark outside. I checked my watch and it read 10:30 p.m. I got off the treadmill exhausted and numb. And the only thing my body cried out for now was sleep.

I had survived the night.

And if you've ever battled addiction or struggled with mental health, you know that sometimes surviving the night is all you can do.

Not long after, I decided to move from Millersburg to a nearby town called Camp Hill and rent an apartment along with a friend of mine. I wasn't far from home and the change in location didn't interfere with my ability to excel in my job, but it helped me immensely. Even just a short distance away, my mind felt instantly clearer. For the first time, I was away from all the reminders of the life I had once lived. Away from the dark, smoky rooms at The Legion. Away from the hills I sped through in my drug-induced mania. Away from the street corners that I stumbled over as my body walked the line between consciousness and total blackout. I felt calmer and happier.

I will always think of Camp Hill as my rehab center of sorts. It was similar to Millersburg, only a bit bigger. There was a shopping mall, numerous places to eat, coffee shops, gyms, and a bookstore. It was a wealthy town, with clean streets and happy, productive people. Everyone seemed to walk with purpose, as if they had somewhere to go and something to do. And while I had a few friends in the area, I could walk the town without running into a single person I knew. No one called out my name or watched me. No one stopped me to talk. No one knew who I was or who my parents were. No one knew my story or even cared. I was nothing but a random guy in a small Pennsylvania town, and that felt good.

My job involved manual labor, overseeing crews of men, and paperwork which I disliked with a passion. I set up in the local Barnes & Noble to tackle a large stack of paperwork one particular day and was shocked at what I discovered. As the buzz of conversation hummed around me and the smell of coffee floated in and out, I felt calm and focused. My productivity skyrocketed. I had never worked in that type of setting - Millersburg didn't have anything like it to offer. Barnes & Noble quickly became my new office. Sometimes, I would spend all day there. I would take breaks and wander the aisles, looking at books. I bought quite a few and soon I was reading constantly. I felt most at peace when books surrounded me. They stimulated my mind, not in the volatile, explosive way that drugs had, but in a calm, steady way. And I liked it.

In reality, I probably should have gone to *actual* rehab. I should have immediately found a solid counselor and a group of like-minded people to journey with me through that first year. But I didn't know that at the time. I didn't really understand the battle I was fighting yet.

I just knew that I didn't want to die.

And so I fought through each day. One workout at a time, one book at a time, one meal at a time, one night at a time.

While living in Camp Hill, I devoted everything I had into my work. My mind was clearer than it had been in a long time. It was as if a thick layer of fog had been lifted. The intense lethargy that used to inhabit every fiber of my being had vanished. I was efficient. I had energy. This quickly resulted in me making more money than I ever had. And I loved it.

Money.

More money.

This is success.

I can earn it. I can achieve it.

This is what I was missing all along.

The dollars in my bank account were the rungs of a ladder that I climbed without restraint. Higher and higher. More, always more. In a few short months, I was making more money than I had ever thought possible. The business grew and we did an incredible amount of revenue that year.

I wore that money like a badge of honor. I purchased a nice watch and the shiny surface caught the sunlight and shone like a flashing beam, shouting my success to the world. I bought designer clothes and other jewelry, anxious to create a new persona for myself.

From a drug addict to a millionaire.

I like the sound of that.

From overweight blob to ripped athlete.

What a story.

What a transformation.

Good job, Zak.

Who wouldn't love this story?

That's what I told myself.

And shouted to the world.

I was right. People did love that story. I began posting on social media often and my following grew by thousands. And it felt good. The money in my bank account, the physical changes in my body, the clothing I wore, the way people seemed to look up to me, these were tangible things that I could grab onto and hold. They seemed to quantify my success and prove that I had recovered.

Transformed.

Changed.

And I desperately *needed* that. I think every addict does. You need proof, you need something tangible that you can point to and say, *"See, I'm different. See, I've changed."* Because you live in constant fear that the beast within will find some way to rise up and overpower you when you least expect it. My money, material things, new body, and sudden popularity on social media gave me that.

But when everything was quiet, when my mind wasn't focused, I could still hear the old, familiar voice of Z-Man, reminding me that he was still just a sip away, that he'd never truly left.

In many ways, my time living in Camp Hill was exactly what I needed. The sense of focus and purpose that my career and physical body provided gave me a life raft. It gave me something to hold onto. It gave me a reason to wake up. It gave me the outward appearance of transformation, just enough to make me believe that I really was different, that I wasn't who I used to be.

And in those days, that's all I had. The shiny watch glinting in the sunlight, the sharper, leaner shape of my body, the number on my bank statement. It gave me enough strength to refuse the cravings of my body, to drown out the demons in my mind. Each day was a battle and I learned to love the thrill and the struggle of it.

I'm all better now, I told myself.

I've got wealth, success, and sobriety.

I'm all better now...

Right?

Chapter 13: Beyond Sobriety

There comes a time when the initial shock wears off. The first few months of being sober, perhaps even the first year, is all about the fight, the battle, and the victory. And there's a high to that fight. When your body screams, you scream back. When your mind rages, you force it into extremes through intense work or exercise until it goes silent. And with each passing day and month, you surprise even yourself.

Another day. I'm really doing this.

Another week. I really have changed.

Another month. I really am sober.

For me, life became black and white. Sobriety was suddenly the only metric by which I measured myself and my life.

Sober = Good

Sober = Successful

Sober = In Control

Sober = Healed

Sober = Healthy

Sober = Stable

Sober = Happy

When you come out to the world as an addict, the only thing people really want to know is whether or not you're sober. Nobody asks if you're happy. Nobody asks if you're taking care of your heart and soul. Nobody asks if you're finding fulfillment out of life. And to be fair, you don't really even ask yourself. Your life becomes tunnel-visioned, existing for a sole purpose.

*A purpose which is defined by the **absence** of something in your life.*

And at first, sobriety is the only success that feels attainable. At first, just getting to the end of the day without drinking is an accomplishment. At first, exercising for hours to get through triggers and withdrawals is the only thing you know to do for your health. At first, not doing a line of cocaine to cope with a hard day at work is an achievement. At first, gritting your teeth, putting one foot in front of the other, and waiting for your demons to go away is the only way you know to heal. *At first, you're not even sure you know what happiness is, you just know what happiness is **not**.* But after the withdrawals subside, after the intense ache and emptiness dies down, after the shock that you're *actually* doing the damn thing goes away, the second part of sobriety begins.

For me, the second part began just after my one year anniversary of being sober. I moved back to Millersburg and bought a house on a portion of my family's local property. It was the same house that my grandparents had lived in when I was a child. Our family name is well-known and deep rooted in Millersburg. The thick wooden walls and floors of that farmhouse told the stories of a generation past, lives that had been lived within those rolling, green hills of Pennsylvania. Truth be told, it was more house than I really needed, or even wanted. My family wanted to keep as much history and property within the family as possible. And I wanted to do my share to make that happen. I had money to spare and needed a more permanent place to live. So, I bought the house and land and moved back to Millersburg.

At first, my life seemed just the same as it was in Camp Hill. Slowly but surely, however, I began to notice small changes. The heaviness in my chest came back. I started skipping workouts and found myself unproductive and lethargic. My motivation for work started to wane. I felt tired, exhausted, and uninspired. And I didn't know why.

That old, familiar voice whispered and I noticed it was louder than usual. But I didn't give in. I didn't drink. I didn't get in touch with my old dealer and ask for a hook-up.

I remained sober.

But I wasn't happy.

The needle of my internal compass seemed to wobble this way and that. I couldn't find the same purpose in work or exercise. I kept working, kept making money, kept excelling at my job.

But things just weren't the same.

As soon as I'd get off work, I'd watch movies and eat all my favorite foods.

What the fuck is wrong with you Zak? Why can't you get your shit together?

You're sober. You're financially stable. You've got a big social media following. What the hell is wrong with you?

The truth was that I *had* made a lot of progress in sobriety. I'd made progress in my career. I'd made progress on my physical body.

But I hadn't made any progress on my heart, mind, or soul.

I still didn't know a damn thing about myself. I didn't know who I was or what I wanted in life. I didn't know why I battled the demons that I did. I had achieved sobriety through sheer grit and force. I had silenced the voices by screaming louder. But I still didn't know why they were speaking to me.

And I was tired.

Because, as I said before, there comes a time when the shock wears off. When the excitement dies down. When your DMs and comment sections aren't as full anymore. When people don't think to check in or ask how you're doing. There comes a time when you're forced to walk down the same streets you used to frequent, when you have to face the same people that knew the *old* you, when you have to live within the very environment that shaped everything you came from.

And that's what happened when I moved back to Millersburg. I didn't relapse in sobriety, but I felt as though I made a total emotional regression. I suddenly felt young and insecure. I felt unsure of myself and depressed. I felt like that twenty-two-year-old kid who battled anxiety, who needed liquid courage to even converse with friends at a party. It didn't matter that I had money in the bank and a year of sobriety behind me, I still hadn't matured on the inside. I only knew that I was capable of being sober and making a shitload of money when I was. And that I liked books.

That was it.

The extent of my epiphanies. The extent of my enlightenment. The extent of my introspections.

And I desperately wanted that to be enough. So many people talked about going to rehab or therapy, getting counseling and having profound breakthroughs. It all sounded dramatic and overblown to me. I was a simple, small-town boy and I didn't like the fancy words and complicated sounding explanations for human emotions and behaviors. I thought therapists and counselors were unnecessary, overpriced, and full of shit.

Couldn't it just be enough that I stopped drinking? Couldn't I just be done with it and get on with life? I just wanted to be better, to be okay. I wanted the problem of my addiction solved, to put it behind me. I had erased as many remnants or indications from my body as I could, at least the parts that other people could see. I had lost the weight and the puffiness from my face and the dullness in my eyes.

But my sinus passageways were still damaged from snorting drugs and the molars in the back of my mouth rotted. My arms still bore the scars of the blades that I had plunged into my own flesh. I wore long sleeved shirts so no one could see them. To me, that seemed to be enough of a fix for the problem. *Done, covered, not relevant anymore.* I knew that no one would ask to see the inside of my mouth and no one would check my nasal passages. *Fixed, transformed, behind me.* I was earning money. I was making motivational posts on social media. On the outside, I was all better, healed, on the straight and narrow path.

But I was still unhappy. Confused. Emotionally unstable.

I didn't know what else to do. I was sober. I was making great money. I had a house and land. What other measures of success were there? Wasn't this what they said happiness would be? Wasn't this the dream?

So, why were the old feelings coming back? Why did I feel so empty? Why did my emotions plunge and swing from one extreme to another? Why did I dip low and then suddenly swing high? How could I go from consuming work like a starving animal and exercising like a madman and to an almost-couch-potato in just a few short months?

I wanted to think that I was over the finish line, that there was some magical marker that I had crossed, taking me from *the before* and placing me into *the after.* So why did *the after* feel so strange? Why did it remind me so much of *the before*?

I wrestled with these questions. When my house was quiet, when I walked to my truck on cold, misty mornings, when I drove the back country roads until the sun painted the sky, when I lay in bed trying to sleep and the sleep wouldn't come, they always surfaced.

But I had no answers for these questions.

So I waited. Waited in silence, hoping for answers. Or even for the questions to just go away.

And then slowly, but surely, the silence started to speak. And through the fog, things became just a little clearer.

And then a little clearer.

And then a little clearer.

I realized that while there is a clear line between *sober* and *not sober*, there is no line that marks the space between *recovered* and *still recovering*. There is no magical before and after. I realized that it would always be just me and then me again and then me again and then me again. All still recovering. All journeying toward a better version of myself. A hundred new iterations as I evolve, grow, and change.

And for all the fucking clichés that ruin the sentiment, the truth still remains that life is a journey.

So when the shock went away, when the excitement and high died down, when my sobriety began to feel normal, that's what I realized. I was on a journey that was going to take time. A lot of time. I had so much I still needed to learn. I had a lot to discover, unravel, and figure out about myself. I wanted recovery to happen all at once. I wanted it fast, overnight. But nothing good in life ever happens that way.

I realized that I couldn't work and exercise my way into a faster recovery. I couldn't push harder and expect to somehow "achieve recovery" as if it were a promotion or badge. It was just going to take as long as it was going to take. I couldn't trade an obsession for drugs and alcohol for an obsession with work and exercise.

The process of recovery wasn't going to be finished with ridding my body of a substance, learning to make good money, and then calling it a day. Getting rid of the drugs and alcohol was only the beginning. It just removes the numbing agent enough for feeling to return. And that's when you realize you have bleeding wounds that you didn't even know about.

Because you won't ever know where your wounds are if you can't feel the pain that is trying to show you where to find them.

Though I had been sober a whole year, I still didn't understand myself. I didn't understand why my internal mental landscape was a battlefield. I didn't understand why my emotions swelled and spilled out unpredictably, triggered by things I couldn't see or understand.

I had taken immense pride in the fact that I had made my journey to sobriety all by myself. Every lonely, sleepless night when I sat at home without anyone to talk to or laugh with. Every time my skin had crawled and my heart pounded with cravings and I had gritted my teeth and bore the pain. Every time I drove myself to the gym instead of the bar.

I did that.

It was me.

All me.

But maybe, just maybe, I needed someone else to walk the next leg of the journey with me.

Chapter 14: Time to Meet The Real Zak Maiden

My thumb brushed the smooth surface of my phone as I flicked the screen. Images, videos, memes, quotes, smiling faces, and blurry pictures flashed before my eyes in a matter of seconds. My Instagram following had grown significantly and I found myself drawn into the world of social media more and more often. I saw social media as a platform, a place where I could help people who were struggling with the same battles that I had fought. My bio read, *"DMs always open,"* and I meant it. As a result, all kinds of people messaged me and poured out their hearts and souls about everything from addiction to mental health to struggling to come out as gay or bisexual. I tried to be a listening ear and help when I could and I was grateful for the connections that social media created.

But I also found myself spending far too many mindless hours flicking through all those faces and videos and quotes and memes. Flash. Flash. Flash. A constant stream of information. It's incredible, really, how fast our minds can process it.

On this particular day, a familiar name popped up. *Heather.*

"I am taking on a few new life coaching clients. Message me if you're interested," her post read.

I paused.

Heather was someone who I had messaged on and off throughout the previous year. She was a mental health therapist and a few days before I made my final decision to go sober, I reached out to ask her advice on the Keto diet. In the following months as I struggled my way through the first year of sobriety, she was kind enough to pass on nutrition tips and advice as I attempted to exercise and diet my way through recovery.

"Zak, you really should consider getting some counseling."

She said these words to me when I was only a few months sober. She was the first person to just come out and say it to my face. She had watched my sobriety journey through social media and talked to me off and on throughout the process. Even though she didn't know me all that well, she knew my situation enough to know that I needed more than running on a treadmill, working eighty-hour weeks, and trying out new diets.

But at the time, I didn't want to hear it.

I was lean, I was sober, I was making more money than I ever had. I wasn't doing drugs and I wasn't partying.

What could I possibly need a shrink for?

That's what I thought at first.

But I couldn't seem to shake the funk that had come over me since moving back to Millersburg. With each passing day, it became increasingly clear that I wasn't as alright as I thought I was. I was floundering, treading water, and fighting unseen battles in the dark without even knowing who my opponent was.

Her words kept coming back to me over and over again.

"Zak, you really should consider getting some counseling."

So when her name popped up my newsfeed above the words, *"I am taking on a few new life coaching clients. Message me if you're interested,"* it gave me pause.

I wasn't really even sure what life coaching meant, but I was desperate. I thought about messaging her, but that was a bigger step than I wanted to take. So I hearted the post with a quick double tap and moved on. A few hours later, Heather messaged me.

"Hey Zak, I noticed that you liked the post I made about life coaching. If you're interested, I'd love to meet with you and talk more about the process. I think it's something that would be perfect for you."

During that season of my life, I was double-minded, back and forth, and unsure of just about everything. But not that day. Call it desperation, call it some kind of divine guidance. Whatever the case, I went for it, and two days later we sat across from each other for our first session.

I was anxious and shifted uncomfortably in my chair as she started our session. I felt hot. My palms were sweaty and my underarms were wet. My chest constricted under her gaze. I sat on the edge of my seat, hypervigilant. I was on guard, my defenses ready, as if I were about to go on trial. Memories of sitting in class, trying to avoid eye contact with the teacher, came floating back to me as I sat, preparing myself for what questions I might be asked. I wanted to be ready.

Heather saw my sweaty, anxious state but she didn't draw attention to it. She took control of the space and broke the silence with a few thoughtful questions. I jumped like an attack dog at each of them, clamoring over myself to talk, to prove that I already knew the right answers. I listened carefully, trying to figure out what she was after, as if each question was a strategically-crafted test, a chance to pass or fail based upon my answer. I'd respond with what I thought she wanted to hear.

I *needed* her to know that I was doing well.

I *needed* her to know that I knew what I was talking about.

I *needed* her to like me, to validate my choices, to give me a stamp of approval that said, "*You have officially recovered.*"

More than anything, I *needed* to prove all of those things to myself. To show myself that I wasn't floundering or treading water, *that I was okay.*

Because truth be told, I wasn't sure at all. Inside, I was still the same, insecure kid hoping to be liked and accepted by the poolside bullies and having panic attacks through class.

And truth be told, I was still in shock that I had *actually* taken the power from the mighty Z-Man and managed to hold onto it for so long. I was deathly afraid that if I showed any crack in my armor, if I admitted to feeling weak or unsure, everything would come crumbling down.

So I sat in that chair, across from Heather, sweating and fighting for the floor. I interrupted her. I talked non-stop, filling the space with words, hoping that somehow the momentum of conversation would cover me from being truly seen. I could hear the sound of my own voice, ringing throughout the room. So arrogant. So self-assured. Inside, my heart pounded with anxiety and uncertainty.

Still, Heather pushed through. She wasn't derailed by my combativeness. She was honest and kind but didn't tiptoe around my feelings. She didn't peek through the windows of my soul; she came right through the front door and took a seat. She pointed out the things she saw - things that I wasn't even aware of.

She was tough on me, placing the responsibility for my life, actions, and choices squarely on my shoulders. She said things I didn't want to hear, things that didn't make feel warm and fuzzy or better about myself. Even though it hurt, the truth was comforting. Though I desperately wanted to prove to her, to everyone, and to myself, that I had my life together, I knew the truth all too well. That's what made her honest assessment comforting. For the first time, I felt like it was okay to admit that I didn't have all the answers, that I didn't know what I was doing. She didn't shame me for where I was, but also made it clear that she wasn't going to leave me there.

That first conversation was a hard conversation, but by the end I felt seen and understood. I felt like I had someone in my corner who I could trust and respect. For so long, I had felt like I was barely outrunning a storm and that it was only by sheer grit and refusal to stop that it hadn't overtaken me.

And that is an exhausting way to live.

I didn't walk out of my first session with Heather with big answers or grand epiphanies, but I did walk away with the feeling that maybe I wouldn't have to run forever. That maybe I could stand still and face the storm without it overwhelming me.

Later, I asked Heather what she thought of me the day we met and she described me as anxious, flaky, detached, and spastic. Someone who thought they knew everything. She also said that she could see me, the real me, underneath it all. Someone who was hurting, fighting for life. Someone who wanted more.

In return, she asked me what I thought of her and I told her that I thought she was a bitch that day. And then we both laughed.

A spaz and a bitch.

That's where we started.

We continued to meet regularly for the following months. To be honest, I couldn't recount each session with clarity if you asked me to. I don't remember every breakthrough or every word spoken. But I remember the essence of the shifts that took place in my life during those months. For an entire year I had talked and posted about sobriety and what it meant but it only took a few sessions with Heather to realize that I didn't fully grasp it myself.

And here's what I discovered: Sobriety and addiction recovery focus on the *absence* of something. It revolves around what you're *not* doing. Because the one thing, the only thing, that consumes you, is learning to live *without* something.

No more alcohol, no more drugs.

And for a while, just the mere absence of it in your life seems to be enough. At first *sobriety* seems to be the pinnacle of *recovery*.

In reality, it's so much more.

Because living life without alcohol and drugs is only the beginning. The absence of substances in your life simply removes the numbness and fog so that you can actually *see* yourself for the first time. So you can actually *feel* the world around you. And you realize that you've been walking around in a daze for years, sleepwalking through life.

As Heather and I began to consistently meet and work together, I realized that I didn't actually know myself. I didn't have good social skills or coping mechanisms. I didn't have good boundaries or communication. I didn't know what I really wanted in life or what made me happy.

For so long, drinking and doing drugs had been my answer to everything.

Happy? Drink.

Sad? Drink.

Bad break-up? Drink and do a line or two or three of cocaine.

Procrastinating at work? Put it out of your mind and drink.

Don't know how to have a tough conversation with a family member? Drink and text your dealer.

These coping mechanisms began at a young age for me. And they were with me throughout all of my formative years. And that's a powerful thing. Because when you drink, when you do drugs, when you frequently alter your mental state and your ability to think and feel clearly, *you interfere with the growth process necessary to becoming a thriving, healthy adult.*

Everyone goes through difficult things; everyone has ups and down. Everyone has hard breakups, big failures and uncomfortable conversations. Those are the things that teach us about ourselves, about life. They are the stimulus to grow and mature.

But drugs and alcohol delay that process.

They allow you to stay in a holding pattern, stuck and stagnant. They keep you wrapped in a hazy bubble of apathy and numbness - not progressing, not maturing, not learning or adapting through struggle. Your body ages under the physical abuse it endures while your mind remains dull, immature, and none the wiser.

I had to come to the hard realization that I had the emotional maturity of someone about ten years younger. Because every time I had been handed a tough situation that could have been a catalyst for growth, I numbed myself, pushed it away, and stuffed it down.

As humans, we have to make mistakes and then reflect on what went wrong. It's how we know not to repeat the same mistake again. As my dad used to say, "The only way you learn is to fuck up."

Because it's that feeling like your life is over when a girl breaks up with you that leads you to understand that you have deeper issues with rejection that stem from something much farther back than a dating relationship.

It's the gnawing sense of emptiness and sadness that helps you understand that you're living a life that leaves you unfulfilled and it's time to change things up.

It's the experience of anger and frustration bubbling to the surface that tells you that you have something you need to deal with.

Nobody likes feeling regret, rejection, sadness, or pain. But they are the clues that lead us to a greater understanding of ourselves and the world at large. They shape us and form us into who we are.

Unless you choose to numb the stimulus so that you can't even feel it.

And that's exactly what I did.

When I felt emotions of any kind, I made them go away with alcohol and drugs, never realizing that I was walking around with open wounds and bleeding scars that needed to be dealt with. When I felt a gnawing emptiness inside, I found ways to make the sensation go away instead of allowing it to show me that I needed to make some major changes in my life. When I was overcome by anxiety at the thought of trying new things, I just knocked myself out instead of pressing past the discomfort and learning to overcome my fears. As a result, alcohol and drugs filled up the space where growth should have been taking place.

They made it perfectly okay to just sit still and stay the same. They made it okay to never grow, learn, and change. They made it okay to repeat the same mistakes over and over and over again. They made it okay to never break bad patterns, never progress, never become anything more than the same version of yourself that you've always been.

Because no matter how much you loathe yourself in quiet car rides when you're sober, no matter how many times you're ashamed for the ways you've hurt someone, and no matter how many times you say you want to become a better person, the moment that alcohol and drugs starts coursing through your body, you don't feel any of those things. Instead, you drink and you tell yourself,

"See, you made it another week.

It's Friday night and you're feeling good. You're not half bad, you little motherfucker, you know that? Sure you make a few mistakes, but who doesn't? You're only human.

Have another.

Live in the moment.

Have another.

See, you don't need change. Aren't you comfortable, aren't you feeling good?

Have another."

And instead of facing your mistakes when you've hurt someone, you drink until the guilt and the shame turn into a voice that says,

"What you did to her wasn't your fault. She's a bitch anyway!

You don't deserve to feel like this.

Have another.

And you know what? Fuck her!

Have another.

You don't need to change a thing about yourself.

Have another.

Have another."

Drugs and alcohol make it okay to remain stagnant. To avoid your mistakes. To run around the toxic hamster wheel one more time. Never growing, never learning, never progressing or becoming a better person.

As I began to awake from that state of constant sleepwalking, I had so much to learn about myself. While my mind may have been numb, my body, my heart, and my soul had endured every situation and felt every struggle. The Real Zak was in there all along, watching, listening, and feeling. All that pain, guilt, shame, rage, and hurt was all there. I just hadn't dealt with it or grown through it. Instead, I had avoided it, numbed it, bottled it up and shoved it down.

As Heather guided me through the process of unpacking my past, these pockets of undealt with emotion came spewing out and I had to release them. I had to heal from my wounds. I had to learn how to communicate and set boundaries. I had to discover who the hell I really was. I had to get to know myself for the first time.

During one particular session, I remember Heather asking questions about my childhood. Stories from my past bubbled to the surface... Stories of me being the outcast on the basketball court, the kid who was bullied into paying for friendship at the swimming pool, the high schooler riddled with social anxiety who didn't know how to talk at a party without being drunk. Stories about my parents, about wanting approval. Stories about my first relationships and sexual encounter and how it left me feeling worthless.

She listened. And then she spoke one word.

Rejection.

The common theme in every story is rejection or the fear of it.

As soon as she uttered those words, I felt hot tears well up. I tried to choke back the sobs, but they could not be restrained. I cried. And cried. And cried. With that one word, a hundred situations and scenarios that I had locked away and shoved down came to mind. Everything I had hidden inside and avoided came crashing in.

Ever since I was a boy, all I had wanted was to be accepted. Isn't that what we all want? I wanted to drink beer and be a *real man* like my dad and brother. I wanted to exist beside kids my own age and feel normal instead of awkward and anxious all the time. I wanted to know that I could make real friends instead of constantly buying affection and acceptance. I wanted to be enough for my dad, to make him happy and please him. I always felt like I needed to be more, always more than myself to be accepted.

That's why I felt like I needed Z-Man.

He promised to make me likable and confident. He promised to make me the life of the party, to give me friends. He promised to make me resilient and untouchable. He promised that he could make people accept me and like me. But while I focused on creating a version of myself that I thought others would like, I let a monster grow and inhabit my body. While I chased the acceptance of a hundred people, I missed the entire point of the lesson that life was trying to teach me.

This fear of rejection was not the problem.

The problem was that I did not accept myself.

Because for every odd remark and passive-aggressive comment and unkind behavior I had ever endured at the hands of others, it was nothing in comparison to the physical and verbal abuse I enacted upon myself. The wounds inflicted at the hands of others was nothing compared to the internal flogging I tormented myself with daily.

I realized that I had never dealt with those wounds and fears. I hadn't taken the time to *meet myself*, to get to know The Real Zak, and accept him.

Instead, I made it to a certain point in life and then went into a holding pattern. I allowed myself to be lulled into a dangerous sleep to the tune of an evil lullaby whispering in my ear, *"One more drink. One more day. One more drink. One more day. Survive until your next drink, your next line, your next pill. And then you'll feel alive again."*

That was the cadence I marched to, sleepwalking through what should have been the best years of my life.

I lived for so long compartmentalizing things. I pushed all my thoughts, feelings, desires, hopes, dreams, disappointments, regrets, traumas, and pain into tiny compartments and locked them away, deep in my soul. And then I drank to forget, drank to numb, drank not to care. Until I quite literally forgot, couldn't feel, and didn't care.

Some people would say I have a disease, that I was predisposed to becoming an addict when I was birthed into this world. Some would say it's because of my environment, a learned behavior I picked up without even trying. Some would say that it was a series of poor choices that piled up.

To be honest with you, I don't find it helpful to put labels on it. While aspects of my story are tough and painful, I didn't have extraordinary childhood or unthinkable trauma that turned me into a drug addict and alcoholic. I can't tell you with certainty all the reasons that I became an addict. I would tend to believe that it was a mixture of many things all coming together at once.

I had social anxieties that I desperately wanted to find relief from. I had pain and fears that I refused to tend to. I had an environment that made it easy to reach for the alcohol and drugs. I had members of my family who also struggled with addiction. And while I wouldn't say that any of those things are the sole reason I sunk so deep into addiction, I recognize that all of them played a part.

I could never *blame* or *attribute* my addiction to my fear of rejection or quest for acceptance. But in the absence of drugs and alcohol, my coping mechanisms of choice, I found that I had a shitload of baggage and bottled up pain that needed to be dealt with. Because I was asleep, I was in a holding pattern, I was too numb to know the wounds and baggage I had accumulated. And without my numbing agents, the force and weight of everything I had suppressed hit me like a freight train.

I didn't realize that recovery is about so much more than just being sober.

True recovery is about emerging from the self-induced fog that you've lived under. It's about having the courage to really *feel* all the things you've numbed yourself from for so long.

I remember sitting with Heather on one particular day and robotically sharing memories from my life. I told her about trauma

I had been through as a child. I told her about grabbing the gun and pressing it to my flesh and pulling the trigger. I told her stories that should have been painful, should have felt terrible.

But I told the stories as if I were reciting a book about someone I had never met.

"Zak, do you realize that you have a strong disassociation between your story and the trauma that you carry as a result of it?" she asked. "Do you realize that it's odd the way you can tell these stories without any sense of emotion?"

I had never even considered that. I was so accustomed to living in a disassociated way. How many times had I felt trapped, watching my body do things and my mouth say things that I never intended to? How many times had I tempted death by driving drunk, or shooting a gun while cocaine coursed through me, and felt nothing? No sense of fear, no desire to see to it that I continued to live. How many times had I plunged sharp edges into my skin to feel something, anything, even pain? To feel *inside* my body for just one moment instead of disassociating with it?

With drugs and alcohol, you can live whole nights without even remembering the things you said and did. You even lose control over your body's most basic functions.

As Heather and I worked together, she began to help me rejoin the severed connections that had created my level of dissociation. The more I began to take responsibility for my actions and thoughts, the more I began to accept myself and the more I mended the connections between myself and my choices, story, and pain.

I began to notice that the times when I would become the most defensive and combative with Heather were the sessions in which she was beginning to open doors into rooms filled with pain, trauma, or regret that I didn't want to deal with. She remained strong and undeterred by my defenses. She kept knocking on those doors. And I kept opening them. As I began to reconnect and take responsibility with all parts of myself, even the parts I was ashamed of, I felt things I hadn't felt in so long. I cried hot tears through many of our sessions.

Those tears and those feelings were a necessary part of my recovery.

They were part of me actually meeting and getting to know The Real Zak for the first time.

And that's why I believe that sobriety is just the first step to actual recovery. Sobriety celebrates the *absence* of something in your life. But you can't stop there. You can't just spend your life celebrating a void. You have to dig deeper. You have to feel and heal. You have to clear away the fog and the things you've spent your life trying to avoid. And that's when you can actually celebrate the *presence* of something in your life. And that is the presence of you.

The process of going through my past, healing from wounds I didn't even know I had, and taking responsibility for my own words and actions wasn't an easy one. Sometimes, I felt angry and annoyed at the process. I didn't want to sit with someone and cry and talk about being a kid or things I had been through. I didn't want to own up to my own shit and shortcomings. I didn't want to face the fact that I hadn't emotionally matured or progressed as a healthy adult for whole years of my life. There were times I tried to sabotage it. I put off my meetings with Heather and gave her bullshit excuses on why I couldn't make our appointments. I would text her that I was "just leaving" a job or "running late." But she knew what I was doing.

And she wasn't going to have it. She drew a line in the sand and made it clear that my disrespect for her time wasn't okay. Her honesty and strength pushed me to face what I was doing, face the self-sabotaging patterns that I always seemed to fall back into. And so I kept showing up. I kept pushing through. And beyond the pain and tough talks and the angry sessions and the crying sessions, the fog started to clear.

I started to see my life and my journey accurately. I started to feel the connection between all parts of myself and at peace to let them coexist together. I didn't react and scramble when I felt angry or sad or just a little off. I didn't spiral when I encountered a situation that tapped on my fear of rejection. I stopped swinging from such emotional extremes. My emotions began to even out.

I didn't need to run for hours on a treadmill or workout religiously every day. I didn't need to always go all or nothing in my pursuits. I could just be myself and show up every day for life in the best way I knew how. Some days, I would be tired. Some days, I would be energetic. Some days, I'd throw dumbbells around or run until sweat poured, and other days I'd walk or sit and read for a while. And that was okay.

After choosing sobriety, I lived so long feeling like I was outrunning something. Like I was fighting to stay ahead of the storm. As if I was one skipped workout away from losing everything I had worked for. But I realized that it wasn't a storm I was outrunning, *it was myself.* I hadn't stopped long enough to actually meet myself. I was so busy defining myself as the recovering addict, fighting to succeed by one single measuring stick, that I hadn't even paused long enough to do what I should have done in the first place.

It was time for me to get to know The Real Zak.

Chapter 15: Everything I Ever Needed

In the months that followed my decision to prioritize my emotional health, I began to notice changes. They weren't drastic or overnight. But, as time went on, I began to feel more levelheaded and more comfortable in my own skin. I didn't feel a constant sense of urgency. I didn't feel as if something was stalking me.

I was able to look in the mirror and see clear green eyes staring back at me. I was able to simply *be* in the moment. At peace with myself. At peace with all parts of my story. At peace with all the imperfect, odd, and weird things that make me who I am. And that's when I really started getting to know myself - the plain, sober Zak Maiden. The naked truth underneath all the masks I wore.

Nature and the great outdoors began to appeal to me in a way that it never had before. It was as if I was seeing the world around me for the first time. When you're sleepwalking through life you don't see leaves on trees and the rays of light that paint sunsets. You don't feel the wind or notice the birds flying and singing. My soul started to heal, piece by piece. I could finally just sit, just breathe, just listen to the birds or the wind and watch the world around me. I had never felt so awake and so at peace before.

Oftentimes, I would set off down the little winding road from my house and walk for hours. My mind would clear and quiet. Mile after mile, my feet would keep moving. I would look around, in awe. It was as if the leaves on the trees were showing off their colors in a brilliant display for me. As if the birds were singing louder than usual to get my attention. As if the wind wanted to blow just so I could feel it brush my skin.

"Has this been here all along?" I asked myself. *"Was I just too drunk, too drugged, too busy, too out of it to notice?"*

It was then that I realized how long I had been asleep; how much I had missed.

For the first time, I felt alive. Truly alive. I could feel my pulse. I could hear my breath. The very pulse and breath that I almost put an end to. I often thought of the gun that misfired. I'd think of the cold metal in my hand and how my story shouldn't have ended the way it did. And I would look at the sky in gratitude.

I am alive.

I am breathing.

And that is a miracle and gift.

On one particular day, I remember kayaking on a lake. I paddled out and the sound of the oar pressing into the water washed over me hypnotically.

No anxiety.

No need to hurry or rush.

No reason to fear the quiet or being alone with my thoughts.

And it was marvelous.

Because when you have battled the impulsive thoughts that come with addiction, when you know that the winding staircases of your own mind lead to dark places, when you've lived with demons in your head, you come to fear stillness. You fear your own inner voice, your own thoughts. That's why you need constant motion and movement to fill the void. More things, more noise, more stimulation. But as you take the journey of recovery and make peace with yourself, you don't fear the stillness anymore. And your mind becomes a peaceful place.

I relished that quiet sense of calmness.

I had subjected my body to such unhealthy and extreme stimulation. I had pushed it to go higher and higher and higher and then let it crash. I had dehydrated it, slashed its flesh, and toyed with the edges of its mortality. And I was so disconnected from my body that I didn't even care. As I paddled that day, I felt a drop of rain on my arm. And then another and another. I had always hated the rain, hated the feeling of it on my skin. But that day was different. I sat there and I closed my eyes, feeling the sensation of every drop that fell. Water dripped down my face and body. I didn't fight it. Something passed between my mind, my soul, and my body. Reconnection, mending, healing. The water ran down the scars from where I had cut myself, it poured over the places where the barrel of a gun had pointed. And I could feel every drop. I could taste it. I soaked it in.

I am alive.

I am breathing.

And that is a miracle and gift.

A few months later, another realization hit me. I didn't have any hobbies. I never had any passions in life besides drugs and alcohol. While the pursuit of the sober life had become a core part of my identity, I didn't want my life to be forever marked by *the void of unhealthy things* but instead defined by *the presence of healthy ones.*

I had no idea where to start-- no idea what I even liked or enjoyed besides being outside and watching movies from the eighties. It felt overwhelming to know where to begin. Everything I had ever done for pleasure or enjoyment had been mixed with alcohol and drugs. Every round of golf, every float down the river in a boat, every game of pool. Every sexual experience. Every social gathering.

Discovering life, love, pleasure, and enjoyment outside of the influence of alcohol and drugs proved to be an interesting endeavor. I felt like a child learning to walk for the first time. I didn't know where to begin, but I knew I had to start somewhere. *Anywhere.*

And so I did.

I started by ordering books about everything under the sun -
from how to run a successful pizza restaurant to how to live your best
life. I owned a van and set to working on fixing it up and repairing it
just to see if I enjoyed the process. Was I a car guy? I didn't know. I had
never taken an engine apart, but I figured I could learn. I spent hours
under the hood, taking my time to learn and gain understanding. I
found the process to be relaxing, enjoyable even. It wasn't much, but
it was a start. It was the beginning of me putting pieces back together,
becoming whole, and moving beyond the narrow identity of being a
former addict.

Through the process, my mind and soul began to open to the
possibility that there was a guiding force in my life, a higher power
fighting for me. I had been around people who went to church all my
life. And to be honest, most of them seemed like unhappy, judgmental
Bible thumpers - ready to shame people and tell them what they were
doing wrong in life.

As a result, I came to associate spirituality and belief in God with
people who think it's their job to make sure that nobody says the word
fuck or comes out as gay. That put a bad taste in my mouth. I hated
legalism. I hated hypocrisy. I hated double standards. I hated seeing
people think they were oh so much better than the next person.

But despite my distaste for religion, I couldn't get away from the
fact that I felt something greater than me at work in my life. An unseen
force of good, a divine guidance. At first, I resisted it. I didn't want to
become the judgmental religious people that I had seen throughout
my life. But the more I avoided it, the stronger that sense became that
I was being led, pursued, chased, and protected. I kept running from
the idea, kept resisting it.

Until one day, I just stopped. Stopped running, stopped resisting.

It wasn't on a special day or holy day. It was on a regular
weekday when I took a deep breath and decided to lay down all my

preconceived notions about God and spirituality. I didn't say big words or experience a dramatic conversion. I simply opened my mind and soul and acknowledged the hand and force at work in my life. I suppose you could say that I prayed that day, but my prayers didn't sound like any that I've ever heard before. I talked out loud, as if I was talking to a friend or talking to myself. I said everything I was thinking and feeling. All my doubts, all my fears.

And then I just released it.

Let it go.

Gave it over.

What followed didn't seem supernatural or what most would call transformational. But for me it was everything. I felt enveloped by peace. Total peace.

I thought back on all the times I should have died in a ditch while driving a vehicle, down those winding Pennsylvania roads, drunk out of my mind. The times I waved and shot a gun into the air. The time I actually tried to fire it into my brain. I felt something fighting *for* me. Something pulling me back when I teetered on the edge of destruction more times than I could count.

I fought it, didn't want to believe it. But ultimately I couldn't run from that sense of knowing, in my soul. I accepted that there *was* something out there bigger than I was. I stopped trying to force my recovery, expedite my healing process, shove my way into becoming some idealized, transformed version of myself. I just surrendered. To the process. To God.

Doing so felt relieving more than anything. I had felt so alone for so long, like the sole generator of every bit of forward momentum in my life. And that's an exhausting thing. As I acknowledged that I wasn't alone and that there was an undercurrent of good, a divine power in my life, I felt like a weight had been lifted. So I leaned into it, trusted it.

Suddenly, I didn't feel like I had to have all of the answers. If there was a force of good that had carried me through so many dark and dangerous times, why wouldn't I trust it to guide me, show me each step of the process when it was the right time? And that's when I began to really and truly feel like myself. Unhurried. Unhindered. Uncomplicated. Trusting the process. Trusting that the next steps will always present themselves when the time is right.

This trust in something bigger than myself gave me more peace than I've ever felt before. My manic desire to push myself to extremes in working, exercising, or mastering my recovery process began to settle down. I no longer felt as if I was grasping at the wind, trying to find something to hold onto. I felt solid and sturdy, grounded and rooted.

One day, not long after, I took a walk around my house and looked at all the things I had collected like trophies, spent money on, and thought I needed. Suddenly, it all seemed so empty, so unnecessary. I was so bent on trying to prove that I was okay, that I was successful, that I was healed. I needed more, always more. I thought it would make me happy, make me feel okay. I thought it would give me some tangible proof that I was on *the other side*. Transformed. The success story. But the truth was suddenly clear. I didn't need expensive watches. Or a set of six pack abs. Or more designer clothing. I didn't need to collect more things. I was enough. Just as I was.

The plain ol' real Zak Maiden.

I began to intentionally pare down my possessions and belongings. They felt weighty and cumbersome, like cheap, plastic trophies collecting dust. So I sold or gave away anything that I didn't need. I streamlined my wardrobe. I stopped buying things. The minimalism and simplicity gave me immense peace. Consumerism lost all appeal and I realized how empty the quest for money, fame, and possessions really was. I had spent so many years of my life chasing momentary highs - alcohol, drugs, sex, money, and new things. But none of those things brought me any true fulfillment. It created a monster. And the monster always craves more. It will always demand that the ante be upped. It is a vicious master.

The world will tell you that you need all these things to be happy, to be fulfilled, to be okay.

But you don't.

So I quit playing the game. I gave it a big *fuck you* by selling everything I didn't need and instead began placing value on true connection with people, with myself, and with the natural world around me.

Don't get me wrong, I still work hard. I still love making money and a good bit of it. I have a beautiful house and a nice truck. But letting go of all the excess, letting go of all the clutter and noise, was the best thing I ever did. The simplicity, the beautiful silence was like music to my ears.

I was at peace.

I was awake.

I was myself.

When I gave up drugs and alcohol, I gave up the numbing agent that kept me from feeling what it truly means to be human and alive. And sometimes that means that I feel emotions more acutely than I used to. Sometimes it means having to face ugly sides of myself or my story that I'd rather ignore or deny. Because there is no buffer. Nothing to reach for to dull the pain. No persona to hide behind. No substance to make me forget or lose feeling. No manic momentum created by pushing myself to extremes in exercise or work. No chasing the accumulation of more possessions to fill the void.

There's just me.

The Real Zak.

And you want to know the truth? Life hurts like a bitch some days. Life makes me want to have a drink and snort a line of coke sometimes. Life is just painful and there are many days that I wish I had something to take away the hurt.

But do you know what else is true?

It's worth it.

It's worth it to live awake. It's worth it to feel every bit of this life. It's worth it to experience true peace inside. To have the ability to be quiet and still inside my own mind without fearing what I will find.

This battle between living awake or going to sleep, facing life head on or choosing an unhealthy coping mechanism, being authentic or creating a fake persona, is not something that only addicts deal with.

It is true that the addict's coping mechanisms of choice are *definite*, they are *visceral*. They are the ultimate embodiment of what it means to choose to live numb, disconnected, and in a destructive holding pattern. But the essence of the struggle is something that everyone deals with.

People have all different ways of sleepwalking through life, of pushing reality away, of numbly existing in a cyclical holding pattern. Some people choose food, some choose sex or pornography, some choose alcohol, some choose drugs. Some people bury themselves in work or lose themselves in another person.

*The truth is that anything that lulls you into an unhealthy pattern that you can't break free from, anything that numbs you, anything that keeps you from becoming the best version of yourself, anything that holds you back or holds you down, **is worth breaking free from**.*

Throughout my recovery journey I would often go back to the bars I used to frequent. Most people would tell you that doing so is a bad idea and they'd probably be right. It's definitely not an ideal place for an addict to be. But I *needed* to go back to those places, those dark, dingy rooms where I wasted away years of my life. I needed to look those demons in the eye and show them who holds the power now.

And so I would sit with a bottle of water in the corner and I would watch. Watch the people around me coming and going. Ordering drinks. Talking. Laughing. Getting angry. Staring off into space.

With my senses clear and my mind sharp, I saw things I'd never seen before. I'd see couples come in for a drink holding hands and then watch their eyes wander to meet anyone's but each other's. I would see anger in the face of one person and a world of hurt in another.

And then I would watch the alcohol work its magic.

Shoulders would relax. Tensions fade. Inhibitions subside. And all those human emotions, all those feelings, and all that pain would dissipate as eyes would glaze over and the body would course with the night's dose of numbing agent.

It is easier to face the bottom of an empty glass than to face yourself. Addict or not, people wander into bars looking for so much more than a drink.

Many a night I would sit in the corner of The Legion, looking around and wondering.

Wondering what the walls would say if they could talk.

Wondering what they have seen.

Wondering what stories they hold.

A man finishes his work for the day and knows his wife and children will be waiting for him at home, but he doesn't want to go. He feels like a failure, a disappointment. He's working a dead-end job and it never seems like there's enough money to provide for everyone's needs. And every time he stares into those little eyes looking back up at him, all he can see is a hundred ways he has let them down and a thousand things he'll never be able to give them in this world.

He once had dreams and plans of owning his own company, of making something big of himself and his life. But the wheels started turning and the years started passing and the kids started coming, and he never did anything he planned to do. The fatigue of disappointment mounted until it became too exhausting to make it through the day.

He can't even meet his wife's eyes or pull her close anymore.

What woman would want to be held by a man who can't provide for his own family?

And so when he gets off work, he goes where he always goes. He drives to the same bar he did the night before; he walks up the same flight of stairs, and he inhales the familiar scent of cigarette smoke. The bartender sees his face and begins to move behind the bar.

"The usual?" she asks.

He nods.

"How's it going?" the man in the seat next to him looks his way.

"Oh, you know. Another day, another dollar. Just paying my dues."

"I'll drink to that."

And then he drinks.

He drinks one glass and the edges soften. He drinks another and laughs with the others around the bar at the same stories they've told and heard a thousand times. He orders another and checks his watch. Another half hour and he knows that the kids will be asleep and his wife will be tucked in bed. And so he stays. Because a bar filled with strangers seems safer than the idea of dinner around a table with his family.

He feels hazy when he rises from his seat. Warm and glazed. The edges of the room seem softer now. He slaps the back of the man next to him and mutters something about "not wanting to make the old lady mad," and everyone lets out a chuckle.

He makes his way to the car and he doesn't feel so bad or worthless anymore. Truth be told, he doesn't feel much of anything. His senses are dulled, perfectly prepared to face the silent wall of his wife's back that will be turned away from him in the bed they share. Three empty glasses and he's prepared to face anything. Anything but himself. Anything but his own reflection in the mirror - a sight that reminds him of all the buried dreams, the failed expectations, the days that bleed one into another with nothing remarkable to show, and the legacy of mediocrity that he will leave behind.

Three drinks.

That's all he needs to make it one more day.

And the walls of The Legion remember.

A woman grasps the thick, burly arms of her date a little tighter as they enter the bar.

He's different, better than the last.

She tells herself these words as she watches his eyes slowly grazing down the body of the woman standing in front of them.

She sucks in, hoping that short breaths and constricted belly will make her look smaller and more desirable.

Can I really blame him? Who would want to be with a woman like me anyway?

All the men she's ever been with have all told her the same things. Told her that she isn't beautiful like the others. That she isn't small or cute. That she's lucky to have a man at all. That they can't help it if they look at other women.

The couple makes their way to the bar and she longs for the relief of that first drink. Until then, she can't stand to meet his eyes or feel his touch.

And so, she drinks.

The alcohol burns hot down her throat and spreads through her chest. Her shoulders relax. She sets the empty glass back on the bar counter and it is quickly replaced by another full one. He makes a joke and she hears herself laughing. Laughing like she used to. Another drink and she doesn't pull away when his hands are on those thighs of hers that she hates so much. Another drink and she laughs even more. The room swirls and the world grows fuzzy. Another drink and she holds his arms as they stumble away while he touches her hungrily.

She's too detached to feel ashamed, too numb to wonder if there's another woman out there who also believes she's his. She's too drunk to care. And so their bodies connect in the dark even though they'll hardly remember in the morning.

Five drinks. Five drinks is what it takes to make it through another week of marriage.

And the walls of The Legion remember.

A young man barely over 21 strides toward the bar's edge, his shoulders back. His hands are clammy and his heart pounds but he's hoping no one sees. He's never liked large groups of people and the anxiety of the night looming ahead pulses through him. He orders a round of shots for the group and downs the clear liquid with one gulp. Another round of drinks quickly follows and then another. He's had three drinks by the time twenty minutes has passed.

Isn't this what men do? Was there ever a night that I didn't see a drink in my dad's hands?

He's determined to show the world that he can take it, show the world what he's made of.

Another drink and then he makes his way into the parking lot. Cash is exchanged for that little clear bag filled with white.

Nose down, breathe deep. Rise and feel invincible. Isn't this what men do?

Back inside the bar, he orders another drink, and then another. The room bends and folds, the boundaries blur, and still things move. He smiles and he laughs. He dances and jokes. He orders another drink and then another and then another and then another.

Ten drinks. Ten drinks and a line of cocaine is what it takes to make him feel like he belongs.

And the walls of The Legion remember.

They remember me.

If those walls could talk, they would tell the stories of good times. Laughter, friendship, and community. I will always think of The Legion as a gathering place, a place that in many ways still feels like home to me. But if those walls could talk, they would tell you the story of the people who spent years within those dark borders - drinking away loss, disappointment, betrayal, and pain just like I did. They would tell you of the men and women who climbed those stairs, longing for relief, something to numb the sting of life.

Maybe that's why I returned to The Legion so many times, even after I became sober. Because I wanted to see the room that held the years of my life while I was too numb and drunk to remember. My life and countless others. You could say we reached for alcohol and drugs to avoid pain, to avoid the hard things that life threw at us.

But I think that more than anything, we were just avoiding ourselves.

Avoiding our fears, our fuck-ups, our hurts, our insecurities, our hopes, our dreams, our longings. And so we rabidly reach for something, anything *out there* to make us feel okay, to fill that void inside.

As the months passed and I continued to allow the walls of The Legion to talk to me, allow my recovery process to take its time, and allow my mind, body, and soul to undergo intense renovation, one truth became abundantly clear.

Everything I ever needed was there all along.

I didn't need to grasp at alcohol, drugs, money, fitness, social media followers, or more things. I didn't need to obsess over finding a new relationship or becoming some specific version of success. I didn't need to be an overnight transformation.

I just needed to be at peace with myself. With my creator. With the entirety of my past and with the unpredictable and sometimes slow way my future unfolds.

And that simple realization changed everything.

How many of us reach for something, anything besides what we have right in front of us? How many of us spend our lives stuffing our faces and greedily grabbing for more and more and more? More of anything that will keep up from being still, from doing the work to get to know ourselves, from facing reality.

How many people spend years at the edges of bar counters, sitting on the sidelines, watching their own lives go by?

How many people sit in front of televisions watching people make love, and fight epic battles, too afraid to love the person next to them on the couch, or face the wars within their own mind?

How many people chase money and success, hoping it will make them feel worthy of the love they already had from the people closest to them?

Everything you or I ever needed has been here all along.

That doesn't mean that we don't need others or that we don't need help, because we do. If you aren't in a good place, if you're making poor choices, if you feel like you're drowning, I'll be the first to tell you to *reach out to someone.* Sometimes that's the difference between sinking and swimming. Sometimes that's the difference between life and death. If you go to my Instagram profile, it reads, *"DMs are always open,"* because I know that everyone needs someone when things get tough. We need recovery houses and counselors and excellent rehab facilities. We need therapists and experts and support systems. We need dreams and careers to chase and passions to ignite us.

But hear me say this. *None of those things can ever fix you or fulfill you.* There is no silver bullet that will change your life except this one truth: *Everything you have ever needed has been there all along.*

You can go to every rehab center, you can go on every date, you can chase every career path, you can sit with every therapist, but at the end of the day *you* are the only person who holds the power to make choices for your life, your body, your soul.

You alone have the power to choose.

You alone have the power to change your life.

You alone have the power to find fulfillment, peace, and contentment.

That doesn't mean that you have all the answers-- because you don't. It doesn't mean that you don't need to seek help, because you do. It does mean that you *have to choose your life for yourself.*

And I think that's the truth that so many people spend their life avoiding.

You have to reach out and grab a hold of the life raft. *You* have to face your demons. *You* have to go home and look your wife and kids in the eyes. *You* have to have the uncomfortable conversations with yourself about why you have to compulsively lose yourself in work or in the bottom of the glass. *You* have to take the flying leap beyond your comfort zone and see what lies on the other side.

How many of us spend the better part of our lives running from this?

We think that we just need to make enough money, find a soulmate, get promoted, or have nicer things. We think that the answer is somewhere *out there* when in fact, it's *within us* all along. It's a scary, beautiful truth. One that I ran from for a long time.

I spent years running, chasing anything that would numb that gnawing feeling in my soul that told me that I was missing some major piece of the puzzle. I spent years chasing anything and everything that promised to be *the thing* that would finally bring me fulfillment and peace. I thought Z-Man would give me confidence and belonging. I thought having wealth would make me fulfilled. I thought having a large social media following would make me feel accepted.

But I found more fulfillment, more peace, more sense of confidence and belonging on a kayak in the rain, under the hood of a car with the cool air on my skin, or on a walk in the forest. Because it was about *me* surrendering to the divine - in me and all around me. It was about *me* making the deliberate choices to grab a hold of the help and healing being offered to me.

So get checked into rehab, pursue the career, and find the soulmate. But know that at the end of the day, the only person who can find peace, fulfillment, and belonging is *you*. The only person who can grab a hold of the life raft is *you*. The only person who has the power to take one step and then another on the path to healing and recovery is *you*.

God can chase you. Your family can hold an intervention for you. Every therapist in the country can give you their best counsel. Life can serve you up every opportunity and give you wild success.

Because everything you or I ever needed has been here all along.

Only you can choose what you do with it.

Chapter 16: Not Those People

My purpose in writing this book and sharing my story is not to give you a silver bullet. It's not to tell you something you didn't know. It's not to unveil some new five-step method for sobriety and recovery. It's not to paint a rose-colored version of what transformation looks like or an awe-inspiring *before* and *after* portrait of myself.

My purpose in writing this book is to share my story in hopes that it will help someone out there who is going through what I went through or has a loved one struggling with the same battles I did. I want to tell you that you're not alone. And it's going to be okay. If you open yourself fully - mind, body, and soul - and trust the process, you will make it out the other side.

My other purpose in writing this book is to de-stigmatize the labels that society seems so quick to apply to human struggle.

Alcoholic.

Drug Addict.

Bipolar.

These are labels that could be applied to me. And I would be the first to tell you that they are fitting. I fit the entire profile of an alcoholic and drug addict and many of the attributes of someone with bipolar disorder. I will be the first to admit that I'm an addict. I'll say it to you, I'll say it to anyone. I have absolutely nothing to hide. I am aware that there are addicts in my family and that I may have been predisposed to it. I also know that the town I was raised in is a prime environment for developing addiction. But through my journey of redemption and recovery, I have realized that there is a strong stigma and stereotyping that comes with these words.

Alcoholic: The man who walks through the door of his home, slurring his words and screaming in rage as his wife cowers in the corner because she knows the pain and abuse he will inflict on her in his drunken state.

Drug Addict: The thin woman with rotting teeth sitting on the dirty street corner, mumbling to herself with needle marks in her arms.

Or

Drug Addict: The rich, successful celebrity with money to burn - throwing parties that cost more than cars, banging strippers and popping bottles, chasing thrills and highs.

There are plenty of people who prove these stereotypes to be correct. There are abusive husbands, street-corner heroin addicts, and addicted celebrities.

But there are also mothers who tuck their children into bed and wearily pour themselves a glass of wine and then another and then another and then another and tell themselves that it's normal, that they just need something to take the edge off. But two glasses turn into three or four most nights and dull headaches come the next day and they can't seem to think as clearly as they used to. *I'm not addicted, I'm just a tired mom,* they tell themselves. And yet the promise of that bottle at the end of each and every day is the only thing that keeps them going.

There are the small-towners that come from goodhearted, successful, hardworking families who try blow in the back of a bowling alley because it's something different and cool and breaks up the monotony of another day. They try it again and again. *It's just for fun. It's cool. We're just being young and crazy,* they tell themselves. But the hunger for more becomes vicious and insatiable. They want out, want to be free again, but how? Who will you tell? Who will you go to? And so they battle alone, losing the fight most days.

There are hardworking providers who live for that first pour at five o'clock. They live for that first sip and the dozens that will follow. It's the only thing that makes the daily grind worth it, the only reward for their effort, the only thing that fills the space where fulfillment, passion, and purpose should have been.

Alcoholics walk through grocery stores and sit in church pews and parent children and make money. *Drug addicts* go to high schools and take high-profile meetings in Armani suits and belong to sororities and make your special latte at your favorite coffee shop.

They are mothers and fathers, daughters and sons, sisters and brothers, friends and lovers.

But no one wants to believe that.

We don't want to think that regular, salt-of-the-earth, good-hearted American citizens fit in these categories. We need *other people* who fit the *"alcoholic"* and *"drug addict"* and *"bipolar"* stereotypes to be the cautionary tale that we tell our kids, tell ourselves.

We need alcoholics to look like abusive lowlifes, not the mom next door. We need the drug addicts to look like homeless vagrants with rotting teeth, not the star high school quarterback from a respected family.

We need the assurance that comes from knowing that, *"at least I'm not like **those people**."*

Because mamas want to reassure themselves that their baby would never turn out *like that.* And the man who can't make it through an evening without a drink or two or three needs to tell himself that he's not *like them.* And the mother with the fourth glass of wine needs to promise herself that she's a far cry from becoming anything *like them.*

Sure, there is research to suggest that some people have a predisposition to addiction, that it can be purely physical and genetic. And I'm not here to argue that. But I am here to say that there are so many people who don't fit a stereotype or profile. Who innocently begin down a dark road and wake up to find themselves battling with unhealthy coping mechanisms and bad habits they can't break. Who will they talk to? Who will they ask for help without fear of being labeled "addict" and "alcoholic" and "mentally unstable," branded by all the stereotypes and stigmas these words bring?

We are all just human. We struggle. We struggle to find fulfillment and peace. We struggle to face our demons. We struggle to face *ourselves*. We use alcohol, drugs, money, sex, social media, entertainment, careers, and consumerism to fill the void, to numb the pain. And sometimes we become so dependent on these things that we can't live without them. We become enslaved, controlled, and addicted to them.

When I began to search for books on the subject of recovery, I found that almost all of them revolved around extreme and extraordinary stories. Jail cells and street corners. Needles and gang rape. Homelessness and poverty. And while that resonates for some, it doesn't ring true for the types of struggles that the majority of the population faces.

I wanted to tell my story because I want people to know that addicts and people who struggle with mental health don't always fit the stereotype. I am a small-town boy who came from a good family. I wasn't abandoned or beaten. I wasn't neglected. I'm the kid on the high school basketball team. I'm the next door neighbor who waves at you when I drive by in my truck. I'm the boy who loves his mama.

Growing up, I was the shy kid at the party who wanted to talk. I was the guy who didn't have any understanding of how to deal with emotions or cope with struggle. I was the small-town kid who was bored, who wanted to feel something beyond the mundane life around me. I was the guy who didn't know who he was or what he wanted to be.

The majority of people who are fighting battles with addiction don't live on street corners. But that doesn't mean that they won't end up there. The truth is that any of us, and I mean *any of us,* are just a set of choices away from being *those people.* I remember listening to the "drug talk" at school when I was young. I remember the grotesque pictures of addicts staring back at me. I scoffed and told myself that it wouldn't, couldn't, ever be me. Because that's only what happens to the weird ones, the crazy ones, the messed up ones, the fucking losers.

Those people.

Not me.

We all want to think that we'd never put a gun to our head and pull the trigger. That we'd never drink and drive. That we'd never become addicted. That we have things under control. That we can stop whenever we want.

But the truth is that we all struggle. Some of us struggle with things that others don't. But *we all struggle.* We all have unhealthy means of coping. We all have poisonous tactics to numb the pain.

And that's why I want to destigmatize these terms and these struggles. I want to destroy the idea that addicts are only in jail cells or rehab centers and on street corners. Because far too many people are hiding their battles. Hiding because they feel like they can't be honest about their struggles. Hiding for fear that they will instantly be branded with a label that will follow them for life.

Because once you're "an addict," people start treating you differently. Suddenly, the entirety of your life and identity is defined by partaking or abstaining from a drink or substance. Sobriety becomes the one and only marker of success and failure.

You become *those people.*

Struggling with addiction is something that will forever be part of me. That little voice that reminds me of how good it would feel to have a drink or do a line of blow will never go away. The voice of Z-Man will always be with me. He grows quieter, his power of influence weaker, but he's always there and I have learned to live with that.

But my struggle with addiction is only *one part* of who I am. I'm a businessman, I'm a man who loves his family. I'm an entrepreneur. I'm curious and thoughtful. I have goals and passions and a big life ahead of me.

I'm human.

Just like you.

There are not *those people.* There are just people. People who make good choices and bad. People who face their struggles and people who don't. People who find redemption and people who refuse to look for it.

No matter what your struggles are, you are not a stereotype. You are not a label.

And you are not alone.

You are a living, breathing person with a body, mind, and soul. You have hopes and dreams and plans. You are full of potential.

And while we need more rehab centers and sober houses and therapists and treatment plans, we also need more conversations about the struggles of everyday people. We need to understand that these struggles aren't just battles fought by *those people* in Harlem and Chicago and Hollywood. We need to talk about the small town with rampant drug use. We need to talk about all the hardworking parents and grandparents who are struggling with closet alcoholism and don't know it. We need to talk about the fact that drugs, alcohol, excessive technology, and rampant consumerism are constantly offered to America's youth - promising them easy happiness, confidence, belonging, and a way to cope while no one is providing them with any great alternatives.

We have to wake up. We have to have some honest conversations with each other. We have to de-stigmatize these struggles so that people can stop feeling afraid of raising their hand and admitting that they need help before the problem is out of control.

We need to normalize asking ourselves more questions. Questions like: *Do I feel like alcohol is necessary to have a good time or be socially at ease? Do I feel the need to always have a drink before being sexually intimate? Do I think often about having a drink after work or on the weekend? Do I drink more than three drinks in one night on a regular basis? Do I really still need the prescription drugs that I've been taking for several weeks now? What drugs are young adults in this area being offered? And what conversations are being had about it?*

Just because someone is a stay-at-home mom or a good ol' boy who runs a local shop or a high school cheerleader from a respectable family doesn't mean that they aren't struggling. This doesn't just apply to drugs and alcohol but to mental health as well. Who's asking the retired schoolteacher who lives alone down the street if she's battling depression? Who's asking the seventeen year old boy about his anxiety? Who's checking on the mental state of the dad who puts in eighty-hour work weeks to provide for his family? Who's asking the teenage girl if she's ever contemplated suicide?

Yet again, we're too afraid of the stigma. Too afraid of the repercussions of honestly verbalizing the battles we're facing. No one wants to be branded with words like *depression, anxiety disorder,* or *mental health struggles.*

So instead we say we're fine. Always fine.

Because we're either fine or we're *those people.*

The depressed people.

The addicted people.

The suicidal people.

The people who are society's failures and misfits.

And *that's* the greatest reason I wanted to write this book and share my story. To break the stigmas and stereotypes.

To tell you the story of a small-town kid who struggled with addiction. Who loves his mom and has seen The Office six times and still laughs hysterically every time. Who tried to kill himself. Who came from a good family and played on the basketball team. Who has social anxiety. Who loves lasagna and garlic bread and wants to have a family some day. Who takes long walks and sees life in a weird way.

I have hopes. I have dreams. I have things I want to achieve in life. I want to help build sober houses. I want to show people that they don't need drugs and alcohol to have fun. I want to have realistic conversations with kids in school about drugs and alcohol. I want to love and respect the people around me. I want to be successful at my job. I want to love people and for them to love me back. I want to follow God and trust His guidance for my life. And I want to share my story and make it okay for more people to have honest conversations with themselves and each other.

So fuck labels and stigmas. If you're struggling, I want you to know it's okay to ask for help. I don't care if you're the deacon's wife or the pretty cheerleader or the respected lawyer. I want you to know that you're not alone. That you're not crazy and weird.

That you're not *those people.*

And I want you to know that if you're willing to open your heart and soul, if you're willing to face your inner voices, if you're willing to face *yourself,* you're going to be just fine. You're not screwed up or innately flawed. You're not a freak or a failure.

You're just you, I'm just me. And this is only the beginning.
So, hi. I'm Zak Maiden.

Your son,

Your boyfriend,

Your brother,

Your friend,

You,

And I'm not just a recovering addict.

Made in the USA
Monee, IL
29 December 2021

87499288R00111